City Breaks in Vienna, Salzburg Budapest and Prague

REG BUTLER

In Association with

CITYBREAKS

1991

D1382604

SETTLE PRESS
HIPPOCRENE BOOKS INC.

Text © 1991 Reg Butler
All rights reserved. No part of this publication may be reproduced or transmitted in any form or by any means without permission.
First published by Settle Press
10 Boyne Terrace Mews
London W11 3LR

ISBN (Paperback) 0 907070 70 1
(Hardback) 0 907070 85 X

Published in United States by
Hippocrene Books Inc
171 Madison Avenue, New York
ISBN 0-87052-949-8

Printed by Villiers Publications Ltd
26a Shepherds Hill, London N6 5AH
Covers by Thumb design Partnership

Foreword

As Britain's leading short breaks specialist, we recognise the need for detailed information and guidance for Citybreak travellers. But much more is required than just a listing of museums and their opening times. For a few days, the Citybreak visitor wants to experience the local continental lifestyle.

We are therefore very pleased to work with Reg Butler and Settle Press on this latest addition to the Citybreak series of pocket guide-books.

Reg Butler is one of the pioneers of postwar tourism to Central Europe. As a young courier, he conducted seasons of tours – to Vienna and Salzburg in 1954 and 1955; to Budapest throughout summer 1956; and to Prague in the following year. Since then he has returned many times to the region, writing travel articles for British and American newspapers and magazines.

For this book Reg Butler has collaborated closely with our resident Thomson staff, who have year-round experience of helping visitors enjoy these four cities. We're sure you'll find this book invaluable in planning how to make best personal use of your time.

As well as City Breaks in Vienna, Salzburg, Budapest and Prague, other books in the series cover Paris, Amsterdam, Rome, Florence, Venice, Moscow, Leningrad and Istanbul. Of course Thomson operate to many other cities in Europe and the Americas from departure points across the UK.

THOMSON CITYBREAKS   1991

Contents

Chapter One

Introducing Central Europe

1.1 Journey to the heart of Europe

For centuries Vienna was the heart of Central Europe: capital of the Austro-Hungarian empire, with a wealthy and sophisticated aristocracy that rivalled the life-style of Paris or St Petersburg. Vienna was a major political player on the European stage, where power reached out East to the Russian empire and south through the Balkans to the retreating borders of the Ottoman Turks.

Much of the present-day Vienna dates from the height of that Austrian power, evoking the late 19th century when Johann Strauss was king of the waltz, and when the aristocratic court life revolved around the huge Winter Palace called the Hofburg. This was the central office for the Hapsburg empire, which had 54 million inhabitants, 16 different nationalities, 9 different religions.

Much of that cultural mix survives today, even though Austria of the 1990's represents a mere 12% of the old Hapsburg empire. Vienna itself has 1.5 million inhabitants out of Austria's 7.5 million population. A highly prosperous city, Vienna still keeps its reputation for charm, welcoming two million tourists a year. Indeed, Vienna rates fourth in tourist popularity among the capitals of Europe – following on London, Paris and Rome.

Vienna is a city set to music – from the grandest of opera through ballet and musical comedy to the nostalgia-packed violins and zithers of a night out amid the village wine-taverns of the Vienna Woods. It has a wealth of museums, including the Art History Museum which ranks high among the greatest galleries of Europe. Within the inner city, little has changed since the ancient fortifications were removed in the 19th century, to be replaced by the stylish buildings, monuments and parks of the Ring.

But, although the past is the great tourist attraction, Vienna still plays a lively role as the main gateway of Central Europe. Forty international organisations are active in Vienna, including the headquarters of the oil exporters' OPEC. Vienna is the third largest UN centre in the world. With the postwar borders of Eastern Europe crumbling, Vienna's central position has regained its former dominance.

For the City Break visitor, Vienna can easily be combined with either Salzburg, Budapest or Prague, to make a highly attractive two-centre package. Each of those three beautiful cities can be reached within a few hours by rail or road; or even by river to Budapest.

Which to choose?

Salzburg combines well with Vienna – good sightseeing potential with magnificent *Sound of Music* mountain and lake scenery to contrast with the urban delights of the capital. Indeed, for an open-air holiday, Salzburg is an ideal base for visiting the Salzkammergut or southern Bavaria by day, with music and good restaurants for evening pleasure.

Wherever Central-Europe freaks are gathered together, discussion can turn on which is the more romantic city – Prague or Budapest.

Frontier city between Europe and Asia during the Middle Ages, and an Imperial city in the 19th century, Budapest on the Danube is a splendid capital with architectural excitement, French chic and Austrian indulgence (just see the locals scoffing pastries at the famous café Vorosmarty!).

Often billed as 'Paris of the East', Budapest features an excellent cuisine with good wine and wild Gypsy music.

In Prague, the centre is virtually unchanged in character since the 18th century. That's why they chose Prague for filming of *Amadeus*, the life of Mozart. There is gas lighting in narrow streets which have been beautifully restored. The splendid Town Hall Square rates among the most beautiful in Europe, with an ancient astronomical clock for an attention-grabbing performance every hour.

A walk over Charles Bridge – one of the fifteen Prague bridges which crosses the River Vltava – is like a 20th-century stroll into the Middle Ages, with no traffic permitted to disturb the entertainers and craftsmen who have adopted the bridge as their favourite pitch. Prague Castle, dominating the skyline, was founded in 9th century, and converted to an imperial residence in 14th century by Charles IV, who aimed to make Prague the leading capital of Europe.

A great city for strolling, Prague is the place where any romantic would feel at home. There are candlelit bistro-type restaurants, ancient wine taverns, and cafés where you can just sit in tranquillity and watch the world go by.

On a historic prewar occasion, Britain's prime minister Neville Chamberlain described Czechoslovakia as "a far-off, distant country of which we know so little." In fact, Czechoslovakia has twice the population of Austria. Today, after long years of East-West division, more City Break visitors are combining sightseeing with the fascination of learning more about the changing way of life in what formerly was hidden behind the Czech Curtain.

Of the four cities described in this book, Prague is the

closest to London – 637 air miles, compared to Salzburg 643 miles, Vienna 780 miles, Budapest 913 miles.

When to go?

For all the four cities, May and June are very attractive months. July and August are the tourism high season. September is heavily booked with Conference traffic. Prague – home town of Good King Wenceslas – makes a determined pitch for the Christmas trade. Vienna and Budapest also promote very active winter seasons of cultural events, with wonderful choice for music-lovers.

Language problems? Czech and Hungarian are tough going. Most visitors just learn a few basic words and then give up. In Prague and Budapest, people in tourism and catering business have reasonable command of English. Otherwise, German is the most useful second language. Restaurant menus are most likely to be translated into German – only rarely into French.

1.2 Explore the cuisine

Viennese cuisine is a blend of specialities from all the countries that once made up the Austro–Hungarian Empire, as well as the native Austrian dishes. The culinary flow has been three-way, so that Prague, Budapest and Vienna can offer an interchangeable choice that could be described as Central European cuisine.

Apfelstrudel, Wiener Schnitzel and Sachertorte make a frequent appearance on Czech and Hungarian menus, while Hungarian goulash or pancakes or Czech dumplings are equally available in Vienna. In Salzburg, the cuisine keeps closer to traditional Austrian and German.

On the drinks list, Austria's white wines from the Wachau district of the Danube have fragrant bouquet; much of the new wine – the *Heuriger* – is consumed in wine-taverns on the edge of the Vienna Woods. Otherwise, Austrian restaurants can offer a full range of wines from France, Germany, Hungary and the rest.

In Hungary, the indigenous wines can keep you occupied throughout a holiday, while Czech restaurants rely much more on imports from Hungary, Bulgaria and Yugoslavia. Czech beer is famed around the world.

A Gespritzter is theoretically half-wine, half-soda. Sometimes they go very light on the wine, heavy on the water. However, on a hot day, a Gespritzter is a very refreshing drink. Another popular thirst-quencher is apple juice – Apfelsaft. Fresh orange juice is quite expensive. If you ask for water, they'll normally serve you bottled mineral water which goes on the bill. But tap water is perfectly safe.

If you order tea, you'll usually get a glass mug with warm water and a tea-bag. If you insist on milk, it will probably be condensed.

In all three countries, the coffeehouse tradition is well established. People go to cafés not merely to quench thirst, but to socialize with friends, or to read the newspapers and weekly magazines. Many coffeehouses date back several hundred years and still have a special atmosphere in which to relax and watch the world go by. No-one can outstay his welcome. Just sit back and try coffee and a pastry. Especially in Vienna there's choice of coffee made thirty different ways. But here's a short list which is valid anywhere in Central Europe.

Types of coffee

Melange – Half coffee half milk: probably the most popular variation among visitors; also called Cappucino
Brauner – Coffee with a little milk
Mokka – Very strong, black and heavily sweetened
Türkischer – Turkish coffee (thick, strong and sweet)
Kaffee mit Schlag – Coffee with whipped cream
Doppelschlag – Coffee with extra cream
Portion Kaffee – Pot of coffee and jug of hot milk

Reading the menus

Menus in Hungarian or Czech are bewildering, and it's very difficult to guess anything more than an occasional word like 'salat' or 'papriky'. See sections 4.9 and 5.9 for help in decoding the bill of fare in those languages.

The more up-market restaurants may offer an English-language menu, but German is far more likely. That's easier than trying to decipher the Czech or Hungarian. So here's a basic guide to the German-language menus of Central Europe:

Main dishes:

Brathuhn	Roast chicken
Beinfleisch	Boiled beef
Ente	Duck
Forelle	Trout
G'selchtes	Smoked ham with Sauerkraut
Hendl	Chicken
Kalbfleisch	Veal
Kalbshaxe	Shin of Veal
Lamm	Lamb
Rindfleisch	Beef
Rostbraten	Minute steak with onions
Schinken	Ham
Schweinefleisch	Pork

Vegetables and Side Dishes:

Erdäpfel	Potatoes
Fisolen/Bohnen	Green beans
Kartoffelsalat	Potato salad
Knofel/Knoblauch	Garlic
mit Kraut	with Sauerkraut
Nudeln	Noodles

8

| Reis | Rice |
| Schwammerl/Pilze | Mushrooms |

Desserts and fruits:

Apfel	Apple
Birne	Pear
Erdbeeren	Strawberries
Käse	Cheese
Kirschen	Cherries
Kuchen	Cake
Obers/Sahne	Cream
Salzburger Nockerl	Egg-white soufflé with vanilla sauce
Torte	Layer cake
Zitrone	Lemon

Some cooking terms:

Garniert	Dressed, garnished
Gebacken	Baked
Gebraten	Roasted
Gegrillt	Grilled
Gekocht	Boiled
Geräuchert	Smoked
in Essig	In vinegar
mit Sahne	Creamed
Pochert	Poached

Drinks:

Bier	Beer
Tee	Tea
Kaffee	Coffee
Milch	Milk
Mineral Wasser	Mineral water
Saft	Juice
Wein	Wine

Some Austrian and Central European specialities:

Apple Soup	Apples, cloves, cinnamon, white wine, lemon juice, sugar and extremely thick cream.
Wienerschnitzel	Thinly sliced veal cutlet coated in egg and breadcrumbs then sautéed in butter.
Wienerbackhendl	Boned roast chicken prepared in the same way.
Geröstete	Sautéed potatoes.
Tafelspitz	Resembles boiled beef but the taste is superb.
Goulasch	Beef stewed in onions, garlic, paprika, tomatoes and celery.
Debrecziner	Spicy sausage

Schaschlik	Brochettes of lamb with onion, green and red peppers.
Cevapcici	Barbequed meatballs
Knödel	Dumplings
Marillenknödel	Dumplings with a hot apricot inside.
Topfenknödel	Dumplings with cream cheese inside.
Palatschinken	Pancakes
Apfelstrudel	Thinly sliced apple with raisins and cinnamon in flaky pastry.
Sachertorte	Viennese chocolate cake.

1.3 At your service in Central Europe

Changing Money

In all three countries, you can readily change money and travellers cheques at arrival airports, banks, exchange bureaux and larger hotels. You need to produce your passport. Commission rates vary and can be higher in hotels. Check first. Generally banks deduct a flat-rate minimum commission, making it uneconomic to change small sums of money.

Travellers Cheques

These are a safe way of carrying money but may be difficult to change at night or over the weekend, especially if you're travelling by surface routes to Prague or Budapest. It's best to arrive with a starter kit of Austrian Schillings or any other West-European hard currency to tide you over. Currently Czechoslovakia and Hungary do not allow import or export of their own banknotes, though the rules may change in the future.

Credit cards

These are generally accepted in Austria, especially in centrally located shops. Acceptance is more limited in Hungary and Czechoslovakia, but you should have no problems with major plastic in tourist areas of the capitals.

Eurocheques

Eurocheques are a safe and common method of payment. They can be obtained from your bank if ordered in advance. In all three countries Eurocheques are readily accepted for currency exchange. In Austria they are widely used in shops, restaurants etc when presented with a valid Eurocheque card. In Austria, numerous cash dispensers are open for use by cardholders. Look out for the blue and red 'ec' sticker. Acceptance in shops is more limited in Czechoslovakia and Hungary.

Currencies

The Austrian Schilling is almost identical to Britain's "old-fashioned" shilling – about 20 to the pound. But you can't buy much for a Schilling! Austrian prices are somewhat higher than in Britain.

Coins are of 10 and 50 Groschen, and 1, 5, 10 and 20 Schillings. Banknotes are in denominations of 20, 50, 100, 200, 500 and 1000. The Schilling is usually abbreviated as Sch. or ÖS or AS.

(See sections 4.11 and 5.11 for the Hungarian and Czech currencies).

Phoning home

Calls made from your hotel room are hassle-free; but most hotels at least double the cost onto your bill. To save money, try your luck from a street or Post Office call-box. For international calls from Austria, Hungary or Czechoslovakia: dial 00 and wait for the tone to change; then dial country code (UK 44) + local area code minus the first 0; then the local number. An audible tone will indicate that you need to insert more coins to continue your call.

Phoning from home

City dialling codes from UK are: 010 – then 43-1 for Vienna; 43-662 for Salzburg; 42-2 for Prague; 36-1 for Budapest. Dialling from USA or Canada: 011 – then codes as above.

Electricity

All three countries are on 220 volts. Plugs are Continental-style two-pin. Pack a plug adaptor if you expect to use your own electric gadgets.

Central European Time

All three countries are on GMT plus one hour – the same time zone as most of Western Europe. So Britain is mostly one hour behind, but also gets out of step through choosing different dates to switch between summer and winter times. So take care when adjusting your watch in late March and September/October!

More Information

Austrian National Tourist Offices:
30 St George Street, London W1R 0AL. Tel: 071-629 0461.
500 Fifth Ave, Suite 2009-2002, New York NY 10110. Tel: (212)-944 6880. Offices also in Chicago, Houston and Los Angeles.
2 Bloor Street East, Suite 3330, Toronto, Ontario M4W 1A8. Tel: (416)-967 3348.

Czechoslovak Tourist Offices:
Cedok Ltd, 17/18 Old Bond Street, London W1X 4RB.
Tel: 071-629 6058; 071-491 2666.
Cedok, 10 East 40th Street, New York NY 10016. Tel:
212-689 9720.

Hungarian Tourist Offices:
Danube Travel Agency Ltd., 6 Conduit Street, London
W1R 9TG. Tel: 071-493 0263.
Ibusz, Rockefeller Center, Suite 520, 630 Fifth Ave., New
York, NY 10111. Tel: 212-582 7412.

Chapter Two

Vienna

2.1 Waltz in to Vienna

Vienna conjures up visions of a never-never musical-comedy city of moonlight on the Blue Danube, and of waltzing through the Vienna Woods.

Of course it's difficult for any city to live up to such sugar-coated expectations. The days of an elegant nobility, splendid in fancy-dress uniform, ended over 70 years ago with collapse of the Austro-Hungarian empire.

Yet there is still much elegance and charm in the Viennese way of life. Down Vienna's most fashionable streets – Kohlmarkt, Graben and Kärntner-Strasse – shops can rival the most expensive streets in Paris, Rome or London.

In famous pastry-shops and coffeehouses, the smartly-dressed clientele savours the greatest luxury of all: a leisured indifference to the passing of time.

The Viennese pride themselves on their mastery of the art of living. They enjoy a highly civilised tradition.

The setting favours the old-fashioned civilities. Much of central Vienna looks like a collection of historic stage sets, but well-kept and newly painted. The Vienna of the Hapsburg Empire still dominates the architectural scene.

In late 19th century, medieval walls surrounding the inner city were removed by order of Emperor Franz Josef. In their place, the Ring-Strasse was laid out – a broad, tree-lined series of boulevards encircling the old city, with pleasant parks, squares and sedate public buildings every few hundred yards.

The buildings were solid, meant to endure for evermore. The basic layout remains unchanged. Vienna has not yielded to the postwar passion for ripping down the old and rebuilding with skyscrapers. A citizen of the 'nineties would not be lost in the central Vienna of today.

Winter and summer palaces of the Hapsburgs still call up memories of when Austria was a great power. Schönbrunn Palace, summer residence of the Emperors, was one of Europe's finest royal homes, with 1441 rooms and 139 kitchens.

For the history-minded visitor, Vienna has numerous such palaces and monuments to offer. But the art-lover has an even better time. Over the centuries, the Hapsburg monarchs collected masterpieces from every school of painting.

Their taste was broad. Some members of the Imperial family preferred the Venetian Renaissance and bought a few dozen Titians and Tintorettos; others liked the Dutch masters, especially Brueghel, or bought up Rubens, or cornered the market in Italian primitives.

The buying continued steadily, from Middle Ages until 1918. With folding of the Austro-Hungarian monarchy, the Austrian State took over the collection – one of the world's greatest, rivalled only by the Prado, Louvre and Vatican. Vienna's Art History Museum could keep any art connoisseur delighted for weeks.

Other travellers prefer to make the musician's pilgrimage: visiting places associated with the numerous composers who made Vienna their home.

If pressed for time, that pilgrimage can be settled in one sightseeing stop, by dining at the Griechenbeisl Inn, the oldest eating-house in Vienna.

Established in 15th century, the Griechenbeisel has been the meeting-place for artists, composers and scientists ever since. The walls and low ceilings of one dining-room are entirely covered with signatures of the famous: Beethoven, Haydn, Schubert, Strauss, Brahms, Chaliapin . . .

Vienna still keeps its reputation as a world capital of classical and light music. A performance at the State Opera House is among the great musical memories of a lifetime. If you're aiming for the musical highlights, time your visit carefully. During summer season, the focal-point of classical music moves to Salzburg for the annual Salzburg Festival.

2.2 Arrival & Hotels

From Britain direct flights to Vienna are operated by British Airways, Austrian Airlines and Dan-Air. From the International Airport at Schwechat, there are two bus services: to the City Air Terminal at Hotel Hilton beside the Stadtpark; and to the South and West Railway Stations. Cost: AS 50.

The 11-mile journey to the city centre takes between 20 and 30 minutes. The highway follows the old Roman road into Vienna, parallel with River Danube and passing through a light industrial zone where the most popular product is Schwechat beer. En route there's a golf course, which is also used for trotting races.

Less convenient but cheaper is an hourly train – Schnellbahn, Line S7 – that connects with the Northern and the Central Railway Stations (Wien Nord and Wien Mitte).

A taxi to or from the airport will cost about AS 500,

Central Vienna

In the following list are the most important sites in the central area. Other numbers on the map relate to a more detailed sightseeing guide – "Vienna from A to Z" – published by the Vienna Tourist Board.

Tip for photographers: The symbols after the buildings denote the most favourable times for taking photographs:

☽ = morning,   ☽ = noon,
☾ = afternoon, ☽ = evening.

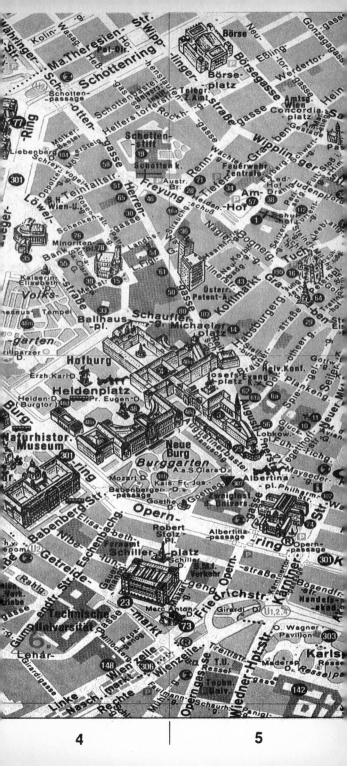

freytag & berndt maps

5

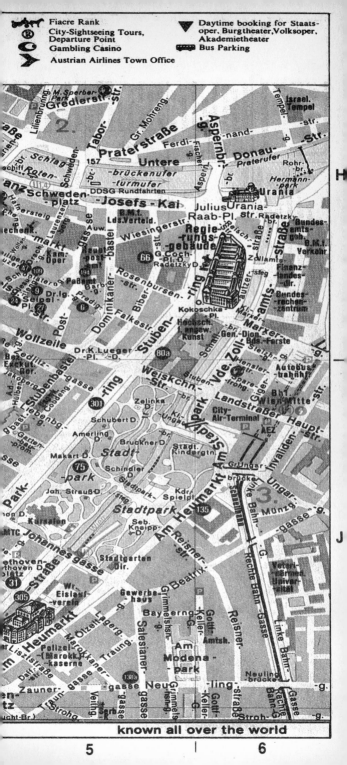

plus AS 15 for each piece of luggage in the boot. On departure from your hotel, it's worth asking about a lower-cost transfer by minibus.

Hotels

Vienna's peak seasons are New Year, Easter, May, June, September, October and Christmas. Lower hotel tariffs are offered from November through March. The most sought-after hotels are those in District 1 – inside the Ring – or on the Ring itself or very close. From these hotels, most of the sightseeing, shopping, restaurants, cafés and nightlife is within walking distance.

For non-central hotels, guests have frequent tram, bus or subway services to the inner city.

2.3 Get your bearings

The original heart of Vienna was surrounded by a massive Ring of fortress walls and bastions which were removed in the 1850's. In their place the Ringstrasse was laid out – a broad tree-lined circle of boulevards, three miles of splendid parks and public buildings on either side. The pattern and style of Vienna today is governed by the Ring, with the Danube Canal shaping the north-eastern segment.

Thus the Ring encircles District 1, the Inner Town which has kept its historic layout, and many of its original buildings. Most of the classic sightseeing highlights are located within the Ring, while the 19th century is represented *on* the Ring in a belt 300 metres wide.

Further out from the Ring is another concentric circle of boulevards called the Gürtel – the Girdle. This encloses Districts 2 to 9, which are helpfully numbered in a clockwise direction. District 2, called Leopolds-Stadt, is wedged between the Danube Canal and the present line of the Danube River itself. Beyond the Gürtel are Districts 10 to 23, which form the suburbs. On the western outskirts are the hills of the Vienna Woods.

Every street-name in Vienna is painted with its District number, to ease the problem of finding where you are. In this book, all addresses outside the Inner City are given with their District number.

Public transport

At the start of your visit, it's worth taking a little time to crack the Viennese transport system, based on an excellent network of trams, buses and subways. Tram No. 1 goes round and round the Ring, clockwise; No. 2 goes anti-clockwise. Subway Line U2 does a half-circle around the Ring, from Karlsplatz (south of the Opera House), to Schottenring (by the Danube Canal).

Most other tram, bus and subway services feed into the Ring, and radiate to the suburbs. *Inside* the Ring there's virtually no public transport, except for a subway stop at the dead-central Stephansplatz. Much of the Inner City is pedestrianized, and most sites are within a five-minute walk of a tram or subway stop on the Ring.

A single-ride ticket costing AS 20 is good for one trip in one direction, including transfers. But most people use advance-purchased tickets which are much more economical. On a City Break the best deal is a 72-hour pass for unlimited travel on trams, buses, underground (U-Bahn) and city trains within the central zone. Cost is AS 102. Timing of the 72 hours starts from date-stamping on the first ride. An alternative is a 24-hour pass costing AS 40; or you can buy four single-ride tickets for AS 56.

These various tickets are sold at tobacconists' shops, marked by a sign "Austria Tabak" in white letters on a red circle, held outstretched by a metal filter-tip cigarette. The tickets are also available at the Transport Information Offices at Karlsplatz or Stephansplatz. Anyone who wants to make more serious use of the Vienna transport system should buy the excellent network map for buses, trams and subways published by the transport authority, price AS 10. All tram stops are clearly named, helping you chart your route.

To validate your ticket with date and time, stamp it in a blue box called an Entwerter either at the subway barrier, or at the front or back of trams and buses. Normally there are no conductors. To get off, press the button by the exit doors. Travel without a valid ticket costs AS 390.

During Vienna's school holidays at Easter, Whitsun and Summer (all of July-August), foreign children under 16 years can travel free.

Taxis

Cab ranks can be found at busy locations and can also be hailed in the street – though whether or not they'll stop is another matter. Watch for the illuminated sign "Frei".

Taxis are costly. The fare is shown by an official meter plus a few Schillings surcharge for inflation. Luggage in the boot costs an extra 10 to 15 Schillings per piece. Tipping is usually 10%.

For a radio cab dial 3130, 6282, 9101 or 4369.

Fiaker (Horse-Carriage) Rides

There are only about three dozen Viennese "Fiaker" left these days. They clip-clop around the city on sightseeing circuits. Some drivers wear the traditional costume of Pepita trousers, velvet jacket and a hat rather like a bowler, called a "Stosser". It's a leisured and stylish way of seeing the sights, but pricey!

Four-passenger Fiakers can be hired at these locations: Stephansplatz; Albertina Platz (behind Opera House); Heldenplatz (by the Hofburg). Settle the price before starting. Reckon something like AS 400 for 20 mins; AS 500 for 30 mins; AS 800 for an hour.

Bicycles

Vienna is well provided with cycle paths. One can cycle throughout the central areas and beside the Danube waterways without having to jostle with motorised traffic. A typical rental price starts at AS 35 an hour. Bikes are available at Salztor Bridge on Danube Canal, phone 4606072 or 327848.

2.4 Basic Vienna

Give yourself six months, and you can see everything in Vienna. Otherwise, on a short city break, at least try to cover the essentials:

(1) Get your bearings with the standard City Sightseeing tour, including Schönbrunn Palace to see how the Hapsburgs lived.

(2) Go shop-gazing along Kärntnerstrasse, Graben and Kohlmarkt.

(3) Relax with coffee and Sachertorte at Sacher's or Demel's, and hang the expense.

(4) Try to get tickets for the State Opera. If no luck, take the daytime tour back-stage or console yourself with the Volksoper.

(5) Have an evening Heuriger tavern-crawl at Grinzing, getting merry on new wine.

(6) Check the colour rating of the Blue Danube by taking a cruise.

(7) Visit the Art History Museum – Kunsthistorische Museum – to see one of the world's greatest collections.

(8) Schedule an afternoon tour of the Vienna Woods, to include Heiligenkreuz Monastery and the hunting lodge at Mayerling.

(9) At noon, watch the performance of the Anker Clock in Hoher Markt for a 12-minute potted history of Vienna with organ music.

(10) Wallow in Johann Strauss nostalgia with an hour at Hubner's Kursalon in the Stadtpark, and enjoy watching Japanese tourists doing the waltz.

Orientation

The introductory city tour helps you get your bearings, with a circuit of the Ring, into the city centre by the Cathedral, a drive across the Danube Canal to the River; and then to the Palace of Schönbrunn, with a guided tour of the apartments, and time to stroll through the Palace park.

Let's follow that routing for sightseeing under your own steam. NOTE: Museum entry times and prices are for guidance, and may change. Most entrances are greatly reduced for children, students and senior citizens. A museum pass costing AS 150 comprises 14 coupons worth AS 15 each. You give 1, 2, 3 or 4 coupons, depending on the fees charged at each museum. The

22

Vienna Tourist Board publishes a pamphlet listing the latest fees and admission times.

Clockwise around the Ring

Starting from the State Opera House, you can walk right round the three miles of the Ring; or take Tram No. 1 (clockwise) and get off anywhere you want to look closer. After dark, most of the buildings and monuments are illuminated. To reverse the itinerary – anti-clockwise – take Tram No. 2.

All the major monuments along the route are 110 to 120 years old, copies of traditional architectural styles from classical Greek onwards.

Opera House – Staatsoper

In 1869, this was the Ring's first building to be completed. It opened to Mozart's *Don Giovanni*. Built in French Renaissance style, the Staatsoper ranks among the world's three leading opera houses, home to the Vienna State Opera and the Vienna Philharmonic Orchestra.

It's an enormous building with audience capacity of 2200. When all lights are switched on, the Staatsoper consumes enough electricity for a city of 40,000. The season of 300 performances runs from September 1 through June 30. Eighty percent of costs are met by government subsidy. See chapter 2.10 for ticket-buying strategy.

For AS 40 you can have a 45-minute English-speaking backstage tour, most days at 10 and 11 a.m. and at 1, 2 and 3 p.m. Check timings, as sometimes tours are cancelled for rehearsals. Morning circuits are best, when there's better chance of going on stage. From 1 p.m. scene-shifters are busy preparing the stage for the first act of that evening's performance; so access to the stage is then less possible.

The Opera House is one of the city's most important focal-points, with a shop-lined underpass leading to the nearest U-Bahn station of Karlsplatz. Alongside runs the principal axis of the Inner City, the Kärntner Strasse, a pedestrian shopping precinct through to St. Stephen's Cathedral. Behind the Opera House is Hotel Sacher on Philharmoniker Strasse which leads to Albertina Platz where horse-carriages wait for passengers.

Burggarten

Clockwise round the Ring, there's a monument to the poet Schiller on the left, backed by the **Academy of Fine Arts**. Then, at the corner of the Burggarten (right), Goethe is slumped in an armchair.

Formerly, these Gardens of the Imperial Palace were for court use only. The Burggarten has been a public park since 1918, a popular spot for picnics. Sited amid the trees is the Mozart Memorial, one of Vienna's most delightful monuments, with foreground flower beds in the shape of violins.

Art History Museum – Kunsthistorische Museum

Next (right) is entrance to the Hofburg – the Winter Palace: see later in this chapter. Opposite (left) is a stately trio of buildings around Maria-Theresien Platz. Identical-twin museums in Italian Renaissance style face each other across the small park: Art History and Natural History. Closing off the square in the background is the huge Trade Fair Palace – Messepalast – which originally was built in 1725 to house the Imperial coaches and horses. Central in the park is a monument to Empress Maria Theresa, sitting loftily on her throne with generals, statesmen and musicians at her feet.

The Art History Museum is among the richest in the world, and is particularly famous for galleries of Rubens, Dürer, Brueghel and Italian Schools. The Museum was purpose-built in 1881 to house this magnificent collection, formed by a succession of art-loving emperors who each bought or inherited more treasures. Quite outstanding is the gallery devoted to Pieter Brueghel the Elder. Nowhere else are so many of his paintings grouped together: comic masterpieces, alive with every detail of Flemish peasant life.

Paintings are located on the first floor, up a monumental staircase dominated by a marble group by Canova – *Theseus and the Centaur*. At mezzanine level, among Sculpture and Minor Arts, is the famed golden salt cellar by Benvenuto Cellini. Even without the art-work, the interior of the building is a fantasy. Give your feet a rest in the central coffee bar on the first floor, and drink in the atmosphere.

Open: Tue-Fri 10-18 hrs, Sat-Sun 9-18 hrs. Entrance AS 45.

Volksgarten

The "Peoples' Garden" (right) is the second largest park in the city centre. It's renowned for beautiful rose gardens and is a favourite choice for a Viennese Sunday afternoon stroll. Look for the imitation Greek temple built 1825, and a memorial to Franz Josef's wife Empress Elizabeth.

Parliament

Next building (left) is Parliament, facing the Volksgarten. In neo-Greek style, it is garnished with imitation Greek statues, symbolic of democracy. Pallas Athena – goddess of counsel and wisdom – presides over the fountain outside. The guides say there's no room for her within.

National Theatre – Burgtheater

Past the Volksgarten is Café Landtmann (right) – one of

the four traditional coffeehouses that still remain on the Ring. Formerly there were 36.

The green-roofed building is the National Theatre, built 1888. The original Court and National Theatre was formed in 1776, and was among the most important theatres in German-speaking Europe. Its classical style was influential in development of the German stage.

Tours backstage are scheduled at 1, 2 and 3 p.m. Mon-Sat during July and August, price AS 30. In other months, check by phone 51444, extension 2613.

City Hall – Rathaus

Facing the Burgtheater is City Hall, an impressive neo-Gothic building topped by an 11-ft knight who is the city's "iron man", a symbol of Vienna. Pattern for the Rathaus was the Town Hall of Brussels. Summer concerts are held in the Arcaded Courtyard. The attractive City Hall Park includes statues of two waltz composers: Joseph Lanner and Johann Strauss Senior.

University

On the left is the University building completed in Italian Renaissance style in 1884. Vienna University is the oldest in German-speaking Europe, established 1365. Currently Vienna's student population is around 90,000.

Votive Church

Next (left) rises the neo-Gothic Votive Church, built in thanksgiving for Emperor Franz Josef's survival from an assassination attempt. In front is Sigmund Freud Park, in commemoration of the psychologist who lived close by, in Berggasse.

Danube Canal

Along Schottenring the building resembling an Italian palace (right) is the Stock Exchange, built 1877. Finally the Ring reaches the Danube Canal, and turns along Franz Josef Kai (Quay). This is *not* the waterfront of the main river, which has been straightened and rechannelled as a flood-control policy.

Schwedenbrücke is departure point for local sightseeing cruises. The elderly paddle steamer *Johann Strauss* is permanently moored close by as a floating café and music pavilion.

Stubenring

The tram route turns away from the Canal, into Stubenring, to continue the circle. The former Imperial Defence Ministry with a monument to Field Marshall Radetsky (left) is used as government offices. Radetsky well deserved a monument, being active in the Imperial Army for 72 years.

The next block (left) is the red-brick Academy of Applied Art, a miniature edition of London's Victoria and Albert. Founded 1864, this museum has good collections of porcelain, glass and period furniture. An entire hall is devoted to Art Nouveau. Open: Daily except Tue, 11-18 hrs. Entrance AS 30.

Stadtpark – City Park

Covering 22 acres – largest of Vienna's 800 parks – these landscaped gardens were opened in 1862. Charming little bridges cross the Wien River, Vienna's tributary to the Danube. The Stadtpark features monuments to Viennese musicians, including Schubert, Bruckner and Lehar. Top favourite is a memorial to Johann Strauss. His role as king of the waltz is still honoured daily at Hubner's Kursalon, where one-hour open-air Strauss concerts are given every fine afternoon from Easter till late October; and also every evening indoors.

Several major luxury hotels are located in this area – Hilton and Inter-Continental facing one another from opposite ends of the Stadtpark; and Vienna Marriott and SAS Palais Hotel along the Ring.

Schwarzenberg Platz and Kärntner Ring

Left is a square dominated by a monument to Field-Marshall Schwarzenberg, who played a leading role in the Napoleonic Wars. In the background is a Soviet memorial to men who died around Vienna in the last days of World War II.

From Schwarzenburg Platz to the Opera House is called Kärntner Ring. During the second half of the 19th century, until the end of the monarchy, many of the buildings were private homes of aristocratic families. Mostly these have since been converted into hotels, banks or travel bureaux.

Typically, the stately Imperial Hotel was originally a private residence. The first floor apartment is completely reserved for Very Important state guests. Hotel Bristol opposite was the residence of a wealthy banker from Prague. The Italian Tourist office was previously the home of Emperor Franz Joseph's mistress.

Inner City – Inside the Ring
Hofburg – the Imperial Palace

Originally a medieval castle which grew wing by wing as Austrian power developed, this huge complex of palace buildings was the seat of the Hapsburgs until 1918. Its size reflects the importance of Austria in the great days of the Austro–Hungarian empire. The palace was both the residence and the administrative centre of the Hapsburg dynasty which ruled for over 600 years. Their golden age was the early 18th century, after the retreat of the Turks from the gates of Vienna.

Today the sprawling buildings house offices of the President and the Federal Chancellor; several museums, art galleries and state rooms open to the public; the Spanish Riding School; and the Court Chapel where the Vienna Boys' Choir sings Sunday mass. Other parts of the complex are used as offices or private apartments. Thanks to its long history the Hofburg is an architectural assortment of Gothic, Renaissance, Baroque and Rococo.

There are several possible entrances. Let's start through the **Palace Gates** on the Ring, into **Heldenplatz** – Heroes Square. The Palace Gates themselves comprise a World War I memorial to the Unknown Soldier. On the right is an equestrian statue of Prince Eugene of Savoy, who defeated the Turks; left is Archduke Charles who triumphed over Napoleon in 1809. In 1938, when Hitler annexed Austria, a giant triumphal rally was held in this square.

Face towards the main palace, and the President's quarters are to the left. Keep looking round anti-clockwise, and you get a dramatic skyline view of major buildings on the Ring: National Theatre, City Hall, Parliament and back to the Museums of Natural History and Art History.

On your right beyond Prince Eugene is the curved facade of the **Neue Burg** – the New Palace – completed in 1913 as an ambitious extension to the main premises. Two museums now occupy the building: Ethnological and Ephesus. The latter museum incorporates turn-of-the-century finds from Ephesus in Turkey, where the Austrian school of archaeology continues to dig. Also on view are collections of Arms – ranking second largest in the world – and of Historical Musical Instruments. (Open daily except Tuesday till 16 hrs. Entrance AS 30.)

Now walk straight on through the main archway into a courtyard with a monument to **Emperor Franz II** (1792–1835). He was married four times, and although Napoleon besieged Vienna twice, he married off his daughter Marie-Louise to Napoleon.

Clockwise around the courtyard, start with **Amelia's Wing** built 1577, and distinguished by a 17th-century clock tower with a normal clock, a sundial, and a moon phase indicator. Next is the baroque-style **Imperial Chancery Wing** dated 1730, with apartments that are included in a guided tour of the **State Rooms**. The tour entrance is at St. Michael's Gate – reached by going straight ahead.

Facing the Imperial Chancery Wing is **Leopold's Wing** – the other side already seen from the Heldenplatz – where Maria Theresa's apartments are now used by the President.

A right turn brings you into the **Swiss Courtyard**, the oldest part of the original 13th-century fortified castle. The name comes from the Swiss mercenary guards who manned the gate. Here is public entrance to the **Treasuries** – Schatzkammer – containing the world's oldest collection of crown jewels, still complete and intact as they were by the 14th century. The most prized possession is the 10th-century imperial crown of the Holy Roman Empire. (Open daily except Tuesday till 16 hrs; or till 18 hrs April-Oct. Entrance AS 60.)

From the courtyard a staircase leads to the entrance of the mid-15th century Gothic-style **Chapel** – the Burg-kapelle – where the Vienna Boy's Choir performs. (For admission to High Mass see section 2.7 'Sunday in Vienna').

More archways lead out of the Hofburg into Josefsplatz, with a central monument to **Emperor Joseph II** (1780-1790), who was a son of Maria Theresa. He was a great reformer, and tried to improve the poor standard of living of the farmers.

His grandfather built the beautiful **National Library**, which faces the monument. The facade is typical Baroque.

The Spanish Riding School, 2 Reitschulgasse

A wing of the Hofburg leads off from Josefsplatz and goes along Reitschulgasse into Michaelerplatz. Built in mid-16th century, the wing was later converted into stables for the white Lippizaner horses of the Spanish Riding School.

The world-famed performances are given in traditional costume. Riders wear buckskin breeches and bicorn hats trimmed with gold. Deerskin saddles lie over the horses' gold-trimmed red and blue saddle cloths.

Morning training sessions are normally open to the public from late February until the end of June, and in November and the first half of December. They are held weekdays except Monday from 10–12 hrs. Tickets are sold at the entrance – no reservations – and cost AS 50 for adults, AS 15 children. To get a seat, rather than standing, it's best to start queuing not later than 9.30.

Full-dress performances lasting 80 minutes are mostly on Sunday morning, starting at 10.45 a.m., admission only with pre-booked tickets. During May and June there are additional Wednesday evening performances at 19 hrs. Seat prices range AS 200-600; standing AS 150. Written orders can be sent to Spanische Reitschule, Hofburg, A-1010 Vienna. Do *not* enclose money! Ticket and travel agencies can also procure tickets, but most unlikely at short notice.

During summer season, a few short performances – excerpts from the full programme – are given on Saturdays at 9 a.m. Tickets priced AS 150 plus a service charge are sold only through agencies.

Dates of performances and training sessions are subject to change, so check the programmes. Some city sightseeing tours are planned to include a Spanish Riding School visit, with entrance tickets paid separately on the bus.

St. Stephen's Cathedral

In the heart of the Inner City stands Vienna's most important Gothic building. St. Stephen's Cathedral, with its 450-ft spire, and roof covered by 250,000 glazed tiles, is one of the capital's major landmarks.

Like most cathedrals which took centuries to build, St. Stephen's is a medley of architectural styles. The Giant Gate, and the Towers of the Heathens on either side of the entrance, are 12th-century Romanesque. Then came a wave of building in Gothic style – the tall South Tower, for instance – followed by a short 16th-century North Tower topped by a Renaissance spire. The 18th century contributed Baroque altarpieces.

The North Tower houses the Boomer Bell – the Pummerin, the largest bell in Austria. The original was cast in early 18th century from captured Turkish cannons and was hung in the South Tower. When the Cathedral was bombed and set alight in 1945, the Boomer fell and was shattered. The replacement – diameter 12 feet and weighing 21 tons – is rung on important church holidays only, and to usher in the New Year.

A lift can take you up the North Tower, price AS 40; or you can walk up 343 spiral stairs inside the South Tower to a dramatic viewpoint 246 feet above street level.

Stephansplatz

Stand with your back to the main entrance of St. Stephen's Cathedral. Here is the crossing point of the Inner City's main routes. To get your bearings: Kärntner Strasse is to your left; Rotenturm Strasse right; Graben straight ahead; Singer Strasse behind the Cathedral. Wander along each of those axes and their side turnings, to make a myriad personal discoveries of Old Vienna. The route permutations are endless!

Kärntner Strasse is the Inner's City's most famous shopping street, named after the province of Carinthia (Kärntnen), which borders Italy. No. 41 is Esterhazy Palace, with an apartment still used by the family. But mainly it's a Casino, open daily from 3 p.m., with a fashion salon below. Kärntner Strasse virtually dives below the Ring at the Opera House – a lengthy pedestrian and shopping underpass called Opernpassage – to end at Karlsplatz.

Along **Rotenturm Strasse**, the first building on the right is the Archbishop's Palace, built 1640. A left turning called Lichtensteg brings you to Hoher Markt with its Anker Clock (see below). Streets to the right lead to a good area for shops and restaurants (see section 2.9). Further down Rotenturm Strasse at Fleischmarkt leads to other suggested restaurant areas – the Bermuda Triangle

29

veering to the left; the Greek Orthodox Church and the Griechenbeisl Inn to the right.

The **Graben**, its side streets and Kohlmarkt are at the high end of shopping elegance and price. This area was the southern side of a Roman fortress without a natural line of defence. So Roman soldiers had to fortify their camp by hand, and dug a protective moat – for which the German word is Graben.

Centred in the Graben is the **Plague Column**, a wildly ornate 17th century memorial erected in thanksgiving for final deliverance from the black plague of 1679. On the other side is a monument to Saint Christopher, patron saint of travellers. Underneath is a WC from the Art Nouveau period. It is now one of Vienna's tourist attractions.

In the other direction, **Singer Strasse** leads to **Franziskaner Platz** – one of the most attractive old squares in Vienna with its Franciscan monastery and church, and 17th and 18th century buildings. Further along brings you to the Stadtpark.

Anker Clock

For an entertaining 12 minutes, go to the Hoher Markt just before noon. The Anker Insurance Company erected this decorative clock in 1911. At midday a dozen historic figures or pairs of figures parade slowly across the clock face, with appropriate background music – from Emperor Marcus Aurelius of Roman times through to Joseph Haydn.

Outside the Ring

Karlsplatz

A few minutes' walk from the Opera House, Karlsplatz is an interesting transport focal-point, where three subway lines – U1, U2 and U4 – intersect. Vienna's underground rail system dates from 1900, when Art Nouveau was "in". Chief architect for the project was Otto Wagner, who introduced Art Nouveau ideas into every detail of contruction. Several of his station buildings have been restored along line U4 – Rossauer Länder, Stadtpark, Karlsplatz, Kettenbrückengasse and Schönbrunn – a good tourist line!

The Karlsplatz entrance pavilion is a delight, and well worth a picture or two. The setting is charming, in Ressel Park which is surrounded by stately buildings. On the corner of Dumbastrasse is the **Musikverein**, home of the Vienna Philharmonic. Its annual New Year's Day concert is always broadcast around the world. Admission to major concerts is almost impossible, as tickets are mostly on a hereditary subscription basis.

Clockwise, the next building around the park is the **Historical Museum of the City of Vienna**, which can help give deeper understanding to your sightseeing. With pictures, maps etc it surveys Vienna from early times to the present. (Open: daily except Monday, 9-16.30 hrs. Entrance AS 30.)

Then – impossible to miss with its distinctive green roof – comes the **Church of St. Charles Borromeo (Karlskirche)**, which ranks as Vienna's finest baroque church. A masterpiece of the architect Fischer von Erlach, the church was completed in 1737. The foreground pool and the two special columns combine with the elegant facade to make a most unusual monument. Inside, paintings are by Michael Rottmayr.

Further round the edge of the park are buildings of the Technical University.

Follow through to the end of the park, to reach the white cube-shaped **Secession** gallery topped by an ornate golden cabbage. It's dedicated to Art Nouveau, with a famed Beethoven Frieze representing the 9th Symphony on permanent display in the basement. At the entrance counters are publications and prints that cover every aspect of the Art Nouveau era. (Open Tue-Fri 10-18 hrs; Sat-Sun 10-16 hrs.)

Finally – get your bearings – you are now at the beginning of Naschmarkt, the daily retail food market which leads to the Saturday flea market. (See section 2.8.)

Schönbrunn Palace

This splendid summer residence of the Hapsburgs was built between 1696 and 1713, designed by the master architect of Viennese Baroque, Fischer von Erlach. The principal State Rooms in best Rococo style are open to the public on guided tours. (A visit is normally included on standard city sightseeings). One of the great highlights of Vienna, the fabulous Room of Millions is still used for major state receptions. Historically, Maria Theresa and Emperor Franz Josef were among the most famous royal residents. Napoleon lodged here in 1805 and 1809, and his son died in the palace in 1832. In the Hall of Mirrors, Mozart performed at age six.

The adjoining park covers about 500 acres with formal gardens, fountains, vistas and severely trimmed hedges and ruler-straight avenues in the accepted style of Baroque landscape gardening. The park is open daily, free, from 6 a.m. till dusk.

The Imperial Coach Collection is located in the right wing of the palace, near the main entrance gate. (Open Tue-Sun 10-17 hrs May-Sep; 10-16 hrs Oct-April. Entrance AS 30.)

Belvedere Palace

This two-section palace – an Upper and a Lower Belvedere (Oberes and Unteres) – is regarded as Vienna's most splendid example of residential Baroque architecture. The garden setting is stately, with a superb view across central Vienna to background hills of the Vienna Woods. Built by Prince Eugene of Savoy in a wine-growing area outside the city walls, Lower Belvedere was his summer residence, while Upper Belvedere was designed for banquets and other festivities.

Besides being very rich, Prinz Eugene was a brilliant general who defeated the Turks 17 times in battle. Among later residents of the Belvedere was Archduke Ferdinand, whose assassination sparked the First World War. The palace is now an art gallery.

The Lower Belvedere (entrance on Rennweg – Tram K) and its orangery house collections of Medieval Austrian Art, and a Baroque Museum. The Upper Belvedere (entrance on Prinz Eugen Strasse – Tram D) features 19th- and 20th-century Austrian art through to modern times.

Open: Tue-Sun 10-16 hrs. Entrance AS 30. No charge for admission to the grounds.

2.5 Other sights in Vienna

Depending on your personal interests and time available, here are some suggestions for supplementary sightseeing.

Capuchin Church & Imperial Vault, Neuer Markt
Close to Kärntnerstrasse, the Capuchin Church is very modest, almost totally lacking in ornamentation. The Imperial Vault is the final resting place of 139 members of the Hapsburg family. Open: Daily 9.30-16hrs.

Museum of Natural History, Maria Theresein Platz
A fascinating collection of Natural History exhibited in 39 galleries and a domed hall.
Open: Daily except Tue 9-18 hrs. Entrance AS 30.

Sigmund Freud's House, Berggasse 19
This house, faithfully reconstructed and with some original furniture, is a Mecca for students of psychoanalysis. Freud lived here from 1891 until 1938 when the Nazis arrived. Open: Daily 9-15 hrs. Located in District 9, near the Votive Church (U-Bahn Schottentor).

Museum of Military History
In the Armory of Arsenalstrasse, District 3, are valuable collections related to weapons and warfare in Austria, from the Thirty Years' War to the First World War. In the Sarajevo Room, see the bloodstained uniform of Archduke Franz Ferdinand.
Open: Daily except Fri 10-16 hrs. Entrance AS 30.
Near South Station (Südbahnhof.) Trams: D, 18.

Museum of Farriery and Saddlery, Linke Bahngasse 11
Special for horse-lovers, a collection of equine-related
items!
Open: Mon-Thu 13.30-15.30 hrs. In District 3.

Special for art-lovers

Vienna offers great riches in art treasures through the ages,
and has been in the forefront of 20th-century art activity.
Check the month's programme for details of special
exhibitions in the city's numerous galleries.

Academy of Fine Arts, Schillerplatz
On the south side of the Ring, facing towards Opera
House and the Burggarten, this impressive picture gallery
is rich in 17th-century Dutch and Flemish paintings,
especially Rubens.
Open: Tue, Thur, Fri 10-14 hrs; Wed 10-13 & 15-18 hrs;
Sat-Sun 9-13 hrs. Entrance AS 15. U-Bahn: Karlsplatz.

Albertina Collection of Graphic Arts, Augustinerstrasse
Just behind the Opera House, a fabulous collection of
graphic material – drawings, watercolours, etchings and
prints by many famous artists including Raphael, Dürer,
Leonardo da Vinci, Michaelangelo, Rubens and Rembrandt.
The world's largest collection of 1.5 million prints covers
the art of printmaking since it began in the 15th century. A
must!
Open: Mon, Tue, Thur 10-16 hrs; Wed 10-18 hrs; Fri
10-14 hrs; Sat & Sun 10-13 hrs. July/Aug closed
Sundays. Entrance AS 30.

Museum of Modern Art, Liechtenstein Palace, 9 Fürsten-
gasse 1
Devoted to works by 20th-century artists including
Derain, Ernst, Kirchner, Picasso, Warhol.
Open: Daily except Tue 10-18 hrs. Entrance AS 30.
In 9th District along Porzellangasse, Tram D stops outside.

Museum of the 20th Century, Schweizergarten
A branch of the Modern Art Museum, features special
exhibitions of contemporary art. On permanent display in
the statuary garden are modern sculptures including
works by Giacometti and Henry Moore.
Open: Daily except Wed 12-18 hrs. Entrance AS 30.
In 3rd District, by South Station (Südbahnhof). Trams:
D, 18.

The musical pilgrimage

Vienna is supremely rich in memories of the many
composers who lived here. Numerous apartments, preserved as small museums, can be visited. The most famous
and convenient is the Figaro House on Domgasse - two

minutes from the Cathedral -- where Mozart composed *The Marriage of Figaro*. If time is scarce, this could serve as your homage to classical music.

Otherwise, for something more in-depth, be prepared for widely scattered visits throughout central Vienna and the suburbs. Beethoven, for instance, changed address twice every year -- in spring he moved to the country suburbs, in autumn he returned to the centre.

An excellent guided coach tour visits a selection of music-related locations in a half-day circuit.

Mozart Memorial -- "Figaro House", Domgasse 5
Mozart's one-floor apartment from 1784 to 1787. Smartly decorated, and with a few items of period furniture, the rooms exhibit paintings, scores, and sketches for theatre sets.
Open: Tue-Sun 10.00-12.15 hrs and 13.00-16.30 hrs. Entrance AS 15.

Schubert's Birthplace, Nussdorfer Strasse 54
This building where Schubert was born in 1797 comprised a series of tiny two-room apartments. The Schuberts were 14 in family, and Franz was born in the kitchen. Open-air Schubert performances are sometimes given in the court-yard, and there's also a small concert room on the ground floor.
Open: Tue-Sun 10.00-12.15 & 13.00-16.30 hrs. Entrance AS 15.
In District 9, served by trams 37 or 38 from Schottentor.

Haydn's Residence, Haydngasse 19
Among the objects displayed are letters, manuscripts and personal possessions as well as two pianos and the deathmask of the composer.
Open: Tue-Sun 9.00-12.15 & 13.00-16.30 hrs. Entrance AS 15.
Located in District 6. Take tram 52 or 58 up Mariahilfer Strasse; get off at Zieglergasse, ask directions and walk.

Beethoven -- House of the Heiligenstadt Testament, Probusgasse 6
In this 3-roomed apartment in Heiligenstadt (19th District), Beethoven composed his Symphony No. 2. Here, in 1802, he became acutely conscious of his deafness. Looking out from his window he could see the bells ringing at the neighbouring church -- but he couldn't hear them. That's when he made his last Will and Testament, saying that a deaf composer could have nothing left to live for. But he went on living for another 25 years, composing music, hearing nothing.
Open: Tue-Sun 9.00-12.15 & 13.00-16.30 hrs. Entrance AS 30.
By public transport: U-Bahn U4 or U6 to Heiligenstadt; then about four stops on Bus 38A to Armbrustergasse.

Districts 2 and 3

Vienna's 2nd District is wedged between the Danube Canal and the Danube River. Sightseeing interest focuses mainly on the Prater and the Ferris Wheel (see Nightlife section 2.10). Johann Strauss lived for several years in a first-floor apartment at Praterstrasse 54, where he composed innumerable waltzes including *The Blue Danube*. Downstairs is now a McDonald's where they compose hamburgers.

At the Danube River, a very long and thin island splits the present-day main channel. Danube Island was inaugurated in 1881 as a big recreation area, and is well equipped with beaches, cycle paths, playgrounds and sports facilities.

Rearing up on the opposite shore is the 817-ft Danube Tower which includes an observation platform, and then a café and a restaurant which revolve at different speeds. Close by are the huge tower blocks of the Vienna International Center (better known as UNO-City), the home of numerous UN agencies. The adjoining Austria Center Vienna is the city's largest conference hall.

Returning over the Danube Canal it's worth making a detour to see the **Hundertwasser House** in District 3, at Löwengasse and Kegelgasse. This incredible piece of municipal housing is a delightful fantasy in colour and architectural design. Don't miss it! Tram N takes you there.

2.6 Take a trip

Much depends on whether you are on a 3-day or a 7-day City Break. During a shorter stay, there's barely time for just one out-of-town excursion. The top choice is a half-day Vienna Woods coach tour, featuring visits to Heiligenkreuz Monastery and Mayerling. During a longer break, it's worth adding a whole-day Danube cruise.

Vienna Woods

For a budget-priced view of the Vienna Woods, go to Heiligenstadt station (U-Bahn U4 or U6 or Tram D), and catch Bus 38A. The route goes through Grinzing wine-village (see Nightlife section 2.10) and thence to the dramatic viewpoints of Cobenzl, Kahlenberg and Leopoldsberg. For walkers there are innumerable footpaths down from these hilltops. From Cobenzl you can walk back to Grinzing through woods which inspired much of Beethoven's *Pastoral Symphony*. It's also possible to cut across to the rival wine village of Sievering, and thence by 39A bus back to Heiligenstadt.

Coach tours to Mayerling and Heiligenkreuz take a different route, southwards along idyllic valleys much loved by Franz Schubert and his friends. The standard tour includes a stop at a disused gypsum mine used for underground aircraft assembly during the last war, and now developed as a tourist attraction with a boat ride on Europe's largest subterranean lake.

Highlight of the trip is the 12th-century Cistercian Monastery of Heiligenkreuz, beautifully located in the heart of the Vienna Woods about 20 miles outside the city. Some 16 monks remain, devoting themselves to monastery upkeep. Close by is the hunting lodge of Mayerling, where Archduke Rudolf, heir to the throne, committed suicide with his mistress Maria Vetsera in January 1889. Dozens of books have been written about the affair. The return journey along the Schwechat river valley then passes by Baden, famed since Roman times for its sulphurous hot springs. The extensive vineyards of Gumpoldskirchen produce a popular wine.

Blue Danube?

Go to Vienna, without seeing the Danube? That's quite possible if you just stay entirely in the centre, where the only waterway is the uninspiring Danube Canal.

Most travellers want to make their own decision on that controversial question: What colour is the Danube? In fact, Strauss's favourite river is only blue if seen in the right light and with the right colour spectacles. For much of its distance, the Danube is a luscious treacle of brown mud scooped from the Bavarian plains, mingled with greyish-green from limestone deposits of the River Inn.

The most beautiful part of the Danube near Vienna is called the Wachau, which stretches 20 miles between Dürnstein and Melk. This wine district features romantic scenery. At every river bend are smiling villages set among orchards, with age-old churches, monasteries and castles to complete the scenic perfection. At Dürnstein Richard Lionheart was held to enormous ransom on his way back in 1193 from the 3rd Crusade.

Most remarkable is Melk Monastery. Built upon a granite rock dominating the river, the Benedictine abbey occupies the site of a Roman encampment. One gallery alone of the magnificent Baroque building is nearly 200 yards long.

Exploration of this area requires at least a full day – whether by rented car, coach-and-steamer tour, or by public transport. Otherwise, shorter Danube cruises are operated mainly from the landing stage at Schwedenplatz on the Danube Canal, to give an hour or two on the main stream.

2.7 Sunday in Vienna

From midday Saturday until Monday morning, shops are tightly closed, and the centre of Vienna can have a somewhat dead appearance. So, on Sunday, concentrate on general sightseeing and museums (bearing in mind that most museums are closed on Monday or Tuesday). Ask your tour rep for details of coach excursions that operate on Sundays.

For a religious service there is choice of 365 Catholic churches. Consider a short list of the Karlskirche for a service in early 18th-century Baroque surroundings; or St. Stephen's cathedral. Either choice makes an interesting experience.

For non-Catholic services, check with the following phone numbers: Anglican 7131575; Lutheran 5128392; Methodist 786367; Jewish 361655; Islamic 301389.

Vienna Boys' Choir

Seats for Sunday Mass sung by the Vienna Boys' Choir at the Imperial Chapel of the Hofburg should be booked at least eight weeks in advance. Write to Hofmusikkapelle, Hofburg, A-1010 Vienna, Austria. Seats are priced from AS 50 to 180. *Don't* enclose cash, but pick up the reserved tickets at the Burgkapelle before the service, which starts at 9.15 a.m.

Otherwise, try queuing at the Chapel at 4.30 p.m. on the previous Friday when a limited number of tickets are sold. The only remaining chance without prior booking is to queue on Sunday from 8.30 hrs (or earlier) for standing room which is free.

The services are held every Sunday and religious holiday from mid-September till June. Don't expect to *see* the choir! By tradition the singers are out of sight in the choir loft. The Boys' Choir can also be heard (and seen!) at 15.30 hrs every Friday in May, June, September and October at the Konzerthaus. Ticket reservations: Reisebüro Mondial, Faulmangasse 4, A-1040 Vienna. Tel: (1) 588040.

2.8 Shopping

On Monday, with museums closed, you can catch up on shop-gazing. Shop hours are normally Monday to Friday 9-18 hrs; Saturday 9 till 12 or 13 hrs. On the first Saturday of every month, when everyone has a month's salary to spend, shops stay open 8-18 hrs.

Vienna is a window-shoppers' paradise, though most of the luxury items seem pricey by UK standards. Shops in the central district offer a turn-of-the-century elegance, with high fashion at high prices.

Most visitors stroll along the Kärntnerstrasse, linking the State Opera House and St. Stephen's Cathedral with shops all the way. Specially delightful is the atmosphere of the Graben, with its summertime outdoor cafés, street entertainers, luxury shops and an elegant clientele. The Graben and the neighbouring Kohlmarkt are Vienna's Bond Street. (Vienna's Oxford Street is Mariahilferstrasse.)

Specially worth admiring is the craftware: glass, hand-painted porcelain, decorative ceramics, bronze, pewter and silver. Other favourite items are petit point, enamel fashion jewellery and bowls, wrought-iron work and leather goods. If you spend more than AS 1,000 at any store, ask for Form U 34 to claim VAT refund (normally 1/6 of the marked price). The merchandise may not be used or opened prior to leaving Austria.

In this city so preoccupied with the past, many side streets are dotted with stores that deal in antiques, old coins, books and stamps. Antique furniture and objets d'art from Hapsburg times can be found especially around Josefplatz – Augustinerstrasse, Plankengasse, Dorotheergasse and Spiegelgasse.

Regular art and antique auctions are held at the state-run Dorotheum at Dorotheergasse 17, which originally was founded in 1788 as a Pawn Shop. Today the Dorotheum ranks among the great auction houses of Europe. Articles can be inspected Mon-Fri 10-18 hrs, Sat 9-12 hrs.

At the other price extreme is the Naschmarkt flea market, quite close to Opern Ring. It's open every Saturday from 8 a.m. till around 4 or 6 in the afternoon, depending when stall-holders feel like calling it a day. On offer is everything from low-grade textiles to collectors' items like watches and clocks, coins, first-day covers, books, glassware and pottery. People come from all over Europe to look and buy. It's certainly worth an hour or two, especially when most Saturday afternoons are blank for shoppers.

Nashchmarkt is also Vienna's most important and colourful retail food market, open every day with a great selection of fruit, vegetables and all other foodstuffs.

2.9 Eating out in Vienna

The coffeehouse scene

The Viennese ritual of coffee-drinking has thrived ever since 1683, when a retreating Turkish army left behind sacks of mysterious beans. A Pole called Kolschitzky knew how many beans make a beverage, and opened the first coffeehouse. The Viennese did not like the bitter taste of the Turkish drink, so Kolschitzky added cream and sugar. He prospered. Soon the custom of drinking Viennese-style coffee had spread throughout Europe.

The Viennese pride themselves as coffee connoisseurs. They would never dream of merely ordering 'a cup of coffee'. The exact ingredients and their proportions must be specified – coffee, milk, cream, whipped cream – each permutation having its technical name.

For most visitors, the favourite is Melange – half-milk, half-coffee, with an optional dollop of whipped cream. A Cappucino ends up rather similar. Most other coffees are very strong, such as Brauner, Mokka and Espresso. These can be either grosse or kleine – large or small. The coffee is served with a glass of water, to help clear the palate.

Part of the Vienna life-style is to have coffee and cake in the afternoon. Every Viennese has his own preferred coffee house and is very fussy about it. The more elegant establishments are a sedate and leisured bolt-hole to escape the 20th century. Several coffeehouses are very famous and expensive, but there is also wide choice of cafés at more modest prices.

Among the most renowned is **Sacher's**, just behind the State Opera House. The establishment is world famed for its feather-light dark chocolate cake – the Sachertorte, a great Viennese speciality. For Melange and Sachertorte, both piled with whipped cream, you can expect a minimum £4 bill.

In the very up-market street called Kohlmarkt (which means Coal Market) is **Demel's** at no. 14, which is the most old-fashioned coffeehouse in Vienna. Like Sacher's, it is expensive but the atmosphere is delightful. Forget your waistline and sample the beautiful cakes, pastries and savoury snacks served with 19th-century formality. They also sell individually made and boxed chocolates.

Sirk, small and elegant at 53 Kärntnerstrasse, was a former supplier to the court. Less expensive is **Heiner's**, with two branches – at 21 Kärntner Strasse and at 9 Wollzeile – with excellent cakes and pastries, and very good coffee. **Café Mozart** on Albertinaplatz also offers elegance and tradition.

For more exploration of Vienna's café scene, here's a short-list of recommendations – all in 1st District, or very close. They also serve other beverages, and often can provide snacks or light meals from a limited menu.

Large and inexpensive

Café Schwarzenberg, on the Ring facing Schwarzenberger-platz. Menu available. Piano music in the evening.

Café Landtmann, on the Ring opposite City Hall. Large terrace. Famous for its choice of 32 different types of coffee. Menu available.

Café Tyrol, on Albertina Platz. Art deco interior, quiet and pleasant. Small snacks available.

Café Central, on Herrengasse in 1st district. Traditional, frequented by locals. This was the haunt of Vienna's turn-of-the-century intelligentsia. Menu available.

Café Raimund, opposite the Volkstheater. Pleasant, spacious, reasonable prices, and a menu is available.

Café Melange on Lichtensteg, beyond St. Stephens on the left. Very pleasant, and quite traditional.

Café Sluka, right beside the City Hall. Very pleasant, and menu available.

Café Museum on Karlsplatz, opposite Secession. Arty, in art deco style.

Small, out-of-the-way and trendy

Kleines Café, on Franziskanerplatz is small and quiet.

Reasonable prices. No menu, only cakes.

Café Hawelka on Dorotheergasse, just off the Graben. Frequented by academics, artists, writers and students of music and literature. Always full! Closed on Tuesdays. Looks dark and dingy, but full of character and local Bohemian atmosphere. Reasonable prices.

Café Corso, Neuer Markt. Small and friendly, with terrace. Snacks and cakes, reasonable prices.

Café Eiles on the corner of Josefstädter Strasse, near City Hall. Menu available.

Whenever you need refreshment in Vienna, there's always plentiful choice, especially within the Ring. Many coffeehouses are called Café Konditorei, where you can buy chocolates as well as drinks and pastries. Lowest cost are the stand-up coffee-bars where you can have a Mocca or a Brauner – small for 50p, big for £1 – or a Melange for 75p. For comparison, these bars also sell an Achtel (one-eighth litre) of wine, white or red, for 50p.

There are several chains of cafés such as **Aida**, **Janele** and **Bawag** where prices are reasonable. Another institution is the **EduScho** coffee chain, which sells coffee beans and ground coffee, claimed to be the best in Austria. As a taster, they offer a small Espresso for only 30p, or double size for 60p. EduScho is not a place to relax – stand-up drinking only – but it's great if you just want a strong coffee to pep you up.

The lunch scene

A traditional Viennese meal usually consists of soup, meat dish and a sweet. The main meal is normally at midday, but most visitors prefer something light at noon, saving themselves for an evening splurge.

For a quick lunch, watch for the chalked-up day's menu on blackboards outside cafés and restaurants – usually soup and main course for around £4 or £5. If you go à la carte, most main dishes in average restaurants cost about £5. Many park cafés feature reasonably-priced snacks. At hot-dog stands, a pair of Frankfurters with bread and mustard could cost £1.60.

If sunny weather tempts you to a park picnic, you can get supplies from any of the supermarkets. There are two, opposite the State Opera House. At a delicatessen, all kinds of cheese and cold meats are priced Austrian style in units of *dag*, which stands for Dekagramm. 10 dag = 100 grammes, or about a quarter pound. Purchases will be neatly parcelled, ready for a picnic at any of the delightful parks around the Ring. Very pleasant and central is the Burggarten.

The restaurant scene

Vienna offers bewildering restaurant choice of every type and grade. The most traditional eating places are the

'Keller' and the 'Beisl' – cellars and inns. A 'Klosterkeller' – monastery cellar – offers a wider range of wines. There are also 'Heurigen-Restaurants' which are traditional wine taverns found mainly in wine-growing suburbs outside the city – at Grinzing, for example. However, a few are located in the city centre, and call themselves 'Stadtheurige'. They are always very friendly with lots of character, atmosphere and local colour. In addition, Vienna has a wide range of more formal restaurants – luxury, intimate or foreign-cuisine.

Note that some restaurants close during July and August for at least a month.

If you just want to wander round, and drop in somewhere that takes your fancy, there are three central areas of inexpensive bars and restaurants that stand shoulder to shoulder.

Away from the higher-cost establishments of the Kärntner Strasse and Graben district explore the little area behind St. Stephen's Cathedral: along Sonnenfelsgasse, Schönlatern-gasse, and part of Bäckerstrasse. It's a very old part of the city, where good-value restaurants, cafés and wine-bars have tradition, atmosphere and local colour.

Typical is **Figlmüller**'s, who specialise in giant Wiener Schnitzels. It's a small restaurant located in a narrow alley between two parallel streets, Wollzeile and Bäckerstrasse. There's no printed menu: just a blackboard with prices. Figlmüller closes at 15 hrs on Saturdays, and stays closed on Sundays and public holidays. Best to book. Tel: 5126177.

Another little area – quite close – is located around St. Rupert's Church, the oldest in the city, to the left of Rotenturm Strasse. Locals call the district the Bermuda Triangle (Bermudadreieck). It's a network of cobbled streets, lined with cafés, trendy restaurants, Beisls and bars, and is particularly lively by night.

The Spittelberg area, in District 7 behind the Art History Museum is an historic conservation area that is well worth finding. From the Volkstheater, go up Burggasse. Three parallel streets comprise this corner of old Vienna: Gutenberg-Gasse, Spittelberg-Gasse and Schrank-Gasse. Along the cobbled streets, lined with historic houses, is a delightful mixture of Austrian, French and Italian-style restaurants and street cafés. On summer evenings the area has a lively atmosphere, thanks partly to a small local theatre.

For something unusual and intimate, though a bit more expensive, try the very small, old-fashioned Biedermeier restaurant called **Zum ebene Erde zum erster Stock** at Burggasse 13. At ground level and first floor, it's rated among the best restaurants of Vienna.

Restaurant Guide

Following is a short selection of restaurants in the different

41

categories – mostly in the middle price-range of £10 to £20 for a meal.

Keller-restaurants

Augustinerkeller, on Augustinerstrasse facing Albertina Platz. In 'town Heuriger' style, on two floors with live music - violin, accordion, guitar. Excellent food and good value.

Rathauskeller, located in the Town Hall itself. Choice of restaurants, some with music. Elegant and traditional with excellent food and good value.

Piaristenkeller, at Piaristengasse 45 in the 8th district. The best of its type in Vienna, in an old cloister. Zither music, extensive menu, good value.

Esterhazykeller, at Haarhof 1, just off Naglergasse in the 1st district. Cosy, out-of-the-way, with terrace, good food and reasonable prices.

Urbanikeller, on Am Hof, one of the most impressive squares in Vienna. It ranks among the oldest and best Kellers in the city, with traditional cuisine, Austrian wine and music.

Lindenkeller, at Rotenturmstrasse 12. Vienna's oldest restaurant, dated 1435. Terrace, very traditional, no music.

Zwölf Apostelkeller, at Sonnenfelsgasse 3. Historic surroundings in underground gothic cloister. Mainly a wine cellar with snacks such as soup and sausages. No music, apart from the clock.

'Beisl'

Griechenbeisl, Fleischmarkt 11, next to the Greek Orthodox church. Several rooms, but everyone wants to dine where walls and ceiling are covered by signatures of famous guests like Mozart and Beethoven. Excellent food and service, with fabulous atmosphere and zither music. Reservation very necessary. Non-reserved clients can be fitted into the Augustiner rooms, a more recent extension upstairs, with much less atmosphere.

Stadtbeisl, Naglergasse 21 in 1st district, with a summer terrace. Quiet and cosy, with good food and reasonable prices. Lovely atmosphere.

S'Müllerbeisl, Seilerstätte 15. Small, with a cellar restaurant. Good food, value and service. No music.

Glacisbeisl, Messepalast, situated in the main Messe exhibition hall close to the Art History Museum. Inexpensive, very traditional, with all sorts of speciality dishes including vegetarian cuisine.

Vegetarian

Siddhartha, Fleischmarkt 16
Wrenkh, Hollergasse

Other restaurants

Smutny, on Elizabethstrasse. Full of local colour and ambiance, with very simple decor. Noted for its lengthy Viennese menu, excellent draught beer and reasonable prices. Surroundings and waiters seemingly untouched by time!

Gigerl, opposite the British Bookshop on Ballgasse. Small, Heuriger-style, but quite expensive. Good food.

Ofenlock, Kurrentgasse 8, just off the Judenplatz. Very popular, cosy turn-of-the-century atmosphere. Good food, quite expensive.

Paulusstube, Walfishchgasse 7 near State Opera, with garden terrace. Very old and cosy, music, good food, reasonable prices, but slow service.

Carrousel Vienne, Krugerstrasse 1. Quite large, not traditional, but very reasonable prices.

Chains of restaurants

Wienerwald restaurants specialise in modest-priced chicken dishes. Very good value, good food and service.

Naschmarkt – large restaurants with varied menu. Specially good value is the menu of the day.

Nordsee – self-service fish restaurants. Excellent fish, reasonable prices. Also take-away snacks.

2.10 Nightlife

Like all European capitals, Vienna has the usual quota of nightlife, from clip-joint strip clubs to sophisticated international cabaret shows and high-rolling Casinos. Most are located in the central area.

Vienna's famous cultural life reaches its peak during the winter months, with theatre and concert performances virtually every night. The Carnival Season, called Fasching, brings high-spirited masked-ball festivities to January and February.

For music in more popular style, the village suburbs on the edge of the Vienna Woods feature wine taverns where traditional Viennese folk music is played year-round. The custom is to drink new wine – called *Heuriger* – and never mind next morning's hangover!

Traditionally, when the new wine has fermented out, mine host invites custom by hanging a pine-tree branch on a pole outside his door. That is the "Sign of the Bush", a symbol since Roman days of a wine-tavern. Mostly these taverns are family operated, and theoretically they sell only wine from their own vineyards. In practice that is no longer so, but the tradition remains.

The taverns have a centuries'-old charm of their own. Well-scrubbed benches and tables are built solidly of two-inch planks that barely quiver at the most boisterous treatment. On summer evenings, customers sit out in lantern-lit gardens. When nights turn chilly, they migrate into the lime-washed parlours.

Drinking rough new wine is an acquired taste. But you can always order 'old' wine – that is, of the previous year's vintage – for a little extra cost. There are no wine lists. Vintages and years are for the connoisseurs, who frequent the 'monastery cellars' and wine parlours of the inner city. You drink either new or old, red or white, served in quarter-litre tumblers, straight from the barrel. After your throat has got used to the rough edge, life can become very rosy. That's when even the most solemn characters link arms, sing, and buy comic hats.

In the *Heuriger* you hear the authentic folk-songs of Vienna: sentimental or comic, according to the singer's mood. Even to a German linguist, the words are difficult to follow, being sung in the thick Viennese dialect that is baffling as London's cockney to the foreigner.

"Schrammel-music tonight" the larger tavern-owners proclaim. A Schrammel quartet – named after the Brothers Schrammel who popularized this form of music in 19th-century Vienna – consists usually of an accordion player, guitarist, violinist and a singer. The repertoire is traditional. Other taverns feature a zither-player and an accordionist.

Food is available usually in hot and cold buffet style. Just go to the self-service counter, pick what you want, and pay on the spot.

These taverns are concentrated especially in the villages of Grinzing, Sievering, Nussdorf and Heiligenstadt, in the northwest suburbs that merge into the Vienna Woods. They are easily accessible from central Vienna by tram or bus. Go round the Ring to Schottentor. Then take Tram 38 which goes direct to Grinzing, the last stop, in 25 minutes. Wander into any of the taverns on the main street, and stay wherever takes your fancy. Bear in mind that the transport system closes down at midnight. The last tram from Grinzing runs at 11.50. Avoid an expensive taxi journey!

The Prater

Still on the popular level, another centre of Vienna's nightlife is the Prater. Originally a royal game preserve, the vast park was opened to the public in 1766. Stretching to the banks of the Danube, the park is a favourite daytime promenade. By night, everything focuses upon the Wurstel-prater – the Fun Fair. Best evenings for a visit are Saturdays and Sundays. On other nights, the Prater languishes.

Dominating the amusement park is the Big Wheel. It was designed by British engineers, prefabricated in England, and erected in Vienna in 1901. There is nothing wildly thrilling about riding on the Ferris Wheel, despite its melodramatic star role in **The Third Man** film. Movement is barely perceptible, with frequent stops to load new passengers into the cabins. A complete ride can take about 20 minutes, giving ample time to enjoy a magnificent view

44

over Vienna, while poised 220 feet above ground level.
Below are the usual fairground attractions, and restaurant
gardens that do brisk trade in beer, sausages and wine.

Opera and Ballet

For any devotee of classical music, a visit to the State
Opera House is one of life's great experiences. The
Viennese love of opera is contagious. Even those who
normally scorn opera can fall under the spell of this
national institution. Tickets for ever-popular favourites
like "Magic Flute", "Don Giovanni", "Tosca" or "Madame
Butterfly" are usually instantly sold out. But there's
always a chance! For less popular works, tickets are much
easier. An alternative, not so 'glamorous', is to console
yourself with the Volksoper, which specialises mainly in
light opera and the big favourites.

Tickets are available at booking agencies around town
which charge an officially approved 25% mark-up. If a
hotel concierge obtains 'impossible' tickets through some
mysterious source, the mark-up can even reach 60%.

Clued-up travellers dodge these mark-ups by going
direct to the central booking office behind the State Opera
House, by Albertina Platz. On the city tourist map, it's
marked by a black triangle. A sign *Bundestheaterkassen*
points the entrance into a courtyard, to the large and
efficient booking hall, highly computerized.

An indicator board shows whether seats are still on
general sale, or sold out. Often, some seats are left with a
restricted view – for instance in the second or third rows of
boxes; or high up, at the side. Even if you have a terrible
seat, the experience is still worth having. There's nothing
to stop you hearing the music in all its full glory!

The booking office is open Monday to Friday from 8 till
18 hrs; Saturdays 9-14 hrs; Sundays and public holidays
from 9-12 hrs. You cannot advance-buy tickets earlier
than seven days before the performance. Staatsoper prices
go from a maximum of 2500 Schillings down to about 100
AS for seats with minimal view. The Volksoper price
range is from 450 or 600 AS downwards. If you're
continuing to Budapest, you can even buy tickets for the
Budapest Opera.

In the expensive State Opera seats, you'll be surrounded
by elegance. Even in the gallery there are black ties and
dinner suits among the audience. Standing is available at
15 Schillings, but only by long queuing before the
performance.

For classical concerts, there is bewildering variety year-
round: in the Musikverein (home of the Vienna Philharmonic Orchestra) and the Konzerthaus (Vienna
Symphonic), in the arcaded courtyard of City Hall, in the
splendid Palais Auersperg or in the Church of the
Augustinian Friars. Ask your hotel desk or tour rep for the

45

detailed monthly programme published by the Vienna Tourist Board.

Discotheques
Queen Anne, 12 Johannesgasse 1
Open: Fri-Sat 2100-0500 hrs.
Capt'n Cook, 23 Franz-Josefs-Kai 1
Open: Sun-Thur, 20.00-0200 hrs, Fri-Sat 21.00-0500 hrs
Chattanooga, 29a Graben 1
Open: Sun-Fri 20.00-0200 hrs, Sat 20.00-0500 hrs
Club Take Five, 3a Annagasse 1
Open: Daily 22.00-0400 hrs
Gerard, 11 Lederergasse VIII
Open: Daily 21.00-0200 hrs
Jack Daniels, 6 Krugerstrasse 1
Open: Sun-Thur 21.00-0400 hrs, Fri-Sat 22.00-0400 hrs

Night Tours
Travel agencies offer several choices of conducted 'Vienna by Night' circuits. Normally they include several aspects of Vienna: a general tour of the illuminations including the Ring and the Prater, a drink in a traditional coffee house with suitable background music, and possibly Grinzing for Heuriger wine and music. On Wednesday nights it's possible to include an evening performance of the Lippizaner horses at the Spanish Riding School. The more expensive jaunts can include a night club show.

2.11 At your service
Banks and Exchange Bureaux
General opening hours for banks are Monday-Friday 08.00-12.30 and 13.30-1500 hours (17.30 hrs on Thursday)

Exchange Bureaux and Banks open late
Westbahnhof (West Station)   Daily 7-22 hrs
Südbahnhof (South Station)   Daily 6.30-22 hrs
Airport   Daily 6.30-23 hrs
Travel Agencies exchange money during business hours Monday through Saturday. An exchange bureau is open daily except Sundays in the Opernpassage (the underpass by the State Opera House).

Post Office and Telephone
Opening hours: Weekdays 8-12 & 14-18 hrs.
General Post Office: 9 Fleischmarkt 1
Main railway station post offices are open weekends and late at night. Stamps are also sold at tobacconists, souvenir shops and from vending machines in front of most post offices.

Telegrams

The central telegraph office is at 1 Börseplatz.

International Phone Calls

Check the cost of long distance calls from your hotel before phoning as these may be very expensive. Save money by phoning from a Post Office or from a call box.

To call UK, insert at least AS 14 which gives you one minute. Follow the dialling instructions in section 1.3 of this book. If you're making several long-distance calls, consider buying a phonecard or "Wertkarte" at post offices. Cost: about AS 100.

Calls within Vienna

Insert one Schilling coin and dial the number.

Emergency Phone Numbers

Police	133
Fire Brigade	122
Ambulance	144
Red Cross	927101
Emergency Medical Service	
Daytime	531153
Night	5500

Other useful Phone Numbers and Addresses

British Embassy, 3 Reisnerstrasse 40 731575
If you need any other embassy, the hotel desk can look it up.

Vienna Tourist Information, Kärntnerstrasse 38, daily 9-19 hrs. The Vienna Tourist Board produces free maps and listings for hotels, restaurants, museums, and the monthly What's On. They also publish an excellent sightseeing guide "Vienna from A to Z", price AS 30.

Austrian National Tourist Office, Margaretenstrasse 1 (corner of Wiedner Hauptstrasse in the 4th district) – for information about other regions of Austria. Tel: 431 60 813
Open: Mon-Fri 9-17 hrs.

Medical

Should you see a doctor while in Vienna, you will have to pay for the consultation. If you intend to claim an insurance refund, get a receipt both from the doctor and the chemist. If sizeable funds are required to cover medical expenses, contact your tour rep for advice.

Chemists (Apotheke)

For night and Sunday service, all chemists display the address of the nearest Apotheke on duty.

Otherwise, try International Apotheke, 17 Kärntner-Ring 1. Tel: 1550. Open: Mon-Fri 8-12 & 14-18 hrs; Sat 8-12 hrs.

Lost Property

If you lose something, contact the nearest police station. After three days try Vienna's main Lost and Found office at 9 Wasagasse 22. Tel: 31 66 11 0. Open: Mon-Fri 8-13 hrs. The nearest U-Bahn is Schottentor (U2).

News

Regular posh papers cost AS 50, but the Guardian – printed in Frankfurt – costs AS 22 and arrives earlier than papers from London.

Tipping

If some Austrian menu prices make you whistle, they usually include all the obligatory extras such as 10% drinking tax, 10% alcohol tax, 15% service charge, and 10 to 20% VAT. In restaurants, just round off the bill. When service is not included, a 10% tip is normal.

Chapter Three

Salzburg

3.1 Introduction

Music and enchanting city sightseeing combine to make Salzburg an ideal City Break destination. A huge bonus is that Salzburg is gateway to one of Austria's most beautiful scenic regions – the Salzkammergut of idyllic lakes and mountains.

The musical scene operates year-round, to include Carnival (Fasching) with masked balls from early January until Shrove Tuesday, an annual Mozart Week in late January, an Easter Festival, Whitsun Concerts, the world-famous Summer Festival, and so through the year till Christmas. December is marked by numerous Christmas exhibitions and cribs, a Christmas Market in the Cathedral Square, decorations and carols everywhere.

In 1991 the bi-centenary of Mozart's death has sharply focused world attention on the city of his birth. Many chamber performances are given in historical rooms where the prodigy Mozart first astonished his audiences more than two centuries ago.

The Salzburg Festival, running from late July and throughout August, is the greatest highlight of the annual calendar. World radio and TV focuses on the larger operas and orchestral concerts and the great morality play *Everyman*, performed in front of the cathedral. But there are more than a hundred other Festival performances, including serenade concerts by candlelight, chamber music in the Mozarteum, organ recitals in the cathedral, Sunday masses with orchestra and choir at the Franziskanerkirche.

Frankly, if the musical scene is not your prime interest, it's better to go earlier or later to Salzburg, when the city is less tightly jammed.

Any time of the year, there are photogenic scenes almost anywhere you point a camera: within the age-old city streets, along well-tended paths beside the river or on the hills, all within a few minutes of the centre. Take a bus or a coach tour, and glorious mountain scenery awaits, every season with a different face.

Combined in a two-centre arrangement with Vienna, Salzburg and its mountain setting make a relaxing contrast to the urban delights of the capital. Even the journey

between the two cities is a visual pleasure, every mile of the way.

3.2 Arrival in Salzburg

A transfer between Vienna and Salzburg by coach gives you a 4-hour journey through beautiful countryside. Express train from Vienna's West Station (Westbahnhof) takes about 3 hours.

Daily flights from London Heathrow to Salzburg are operated by Austrian Airlines and British Airways. Some tour operators fly clients to Munich, with onward travel by coach.

If you're arriving individually, Bus no. 77 picks up at Salzburg airport – 4 kms from the centre – and goes to the railway station. The service runs every 15 minutes Monday to Friday and every 30 minutes Saturday and Sunday. Journey time: about 15 minutes. Cost: 17 Schillings.

By taxi, the cost into central Salzburg from the airport is around AS 150 for the 10-minute journey. An extra AS 10 is charged for each piece of luggage in the boot. Your tour rep or the hotel may be able to arrange a more economical mini-bus transfer for the return journey.

3.3 Public transport

Salzburg is a relatively small city, most hotels are central, and sightseeing highlights are all within easy walking distance. Many visitors make little use of public transport, except for rides on the Fortress funicular or on the Mönchsberg Lift to the Café Winkler terrace.

However, the bus service in Salzburg is frequent, quick, and easy to use. Single tickets bought from the driver cost AS 17; or you can advance-buy five tickets at AS 11 each. These tickets are also valid for the funicular, the Mönchsberg Lift and on the urban railway – Lokalbahn – as far as Bergheim.

A 24-hour Rover Ticket costing AS 44 – or 72-hour ticket costing AS 80 – is good value for anyone making more active use of the local transport network. Tickets can be purchased at the following offices, which can also provide route maps:
Transport Service Ticket Office – Griesgasse 21
Lokalbahnhof (opposite the main railway station)
Fortress Cable-car Ticket Office
Mönchsberg Lift (from the conductor)
Tourist Office Information Points
Tabak-Trafiken (tobacconists' with special sign – there are 91 of them throughout the city).

Taxis

Taxis are expensive, considering the short distances within Salzburg, and are often hard to find. If possible, avoid using them, especially during the Festival. If you do need a

taxi it's wise to pre-book:
Salburger Radiotaxi Service (Funktaxi-Vereinigung),
Rainerstrasse 27   Tel: 76111 or 77111
Advance bookings   Tel: 74400

Bicycle Hire

Many visitors get a bike for the day, riding along riverside
paths. In summer, with good weather, people go to open-
air swimming pools. There's one about 10 minutes from
the centre, direction Leopoldskron. Or you can cycle to
the Gaisburg, which has pretty scenery. Cost of bike-hire
is about AS 100 per day. Take your passport, needed as
security deposit.
Two addresses:
Main Railway Station, desk 3. Tel: 71541-337 (Apr-Nov)
Tourist Information Office on Mozartplatz.

Horse-cabs

The cab-rank for tourist circuits is in Residenzplatz. The
carriages hold four passengers. For a ride lasting about
20-25 minutes, reckon at least AS 320; for 50 minutes, AS
620.

3.4 Basic Salzburg

If you go overboard on chamber music, Salzburg can keep
you happy every evening, year-round. On a short visit,
here's a check-list on what else to do.

(1)   Wander very slowly along Getreidegasse, shop-
gazing, taking pictures of wrought-iron shop signs and
peeking into side alleys and courtyards.
(2)   Visit Mozart's birthplace at No. 9 Getreidegasse.
(3)   Take the lift to Café Winkler, admire the view; then
walk through hilltop Mönchsberg woodlands to the
Festung and down by funicular – or vice versa.
(4)   At 11 a.m. or 6 p.m. listen to the Carillon on
Residenz Platz.
(5)   At the Marionette Theatre, see puppets performing
to opera music recorded from the Salzburg Festival.
(6)   Get drenched by the trick fountains of Hellbrunn.
(7)   Conjure up memories of *White Horse Inn* or *Sound of
Music* by taking an afternoon coach tour of the Salzkammergut lakes.
(8)   Try the local soufflé speciality, vanilla-flavoured
Salzburger Nockerl.
(9)   Admire the flower displays in Mirabell Garden.
(10) Cross the border to Berchtesgaden, and see where
Hitler built his ''Eagle's Nest''.

Orientation

Almost at the centre of Austria, Salzburg is capital of
Salzburg province on the northern slopes of the Alps. The

medieval riches of the region derived from a salt-mining monopoly – hence the word *Salz* which occurs in the city's name and in the River Salzach which flows through the heart of Salzburg.

Its natural setting is superb. The Romans developed the site as an administrative centre, with one of their main military roads bridging the Salzach. Later, the prince archbishops of Salzburg established mighty power in the land, building a cathedral overlooked by a massive hilltop fortress. Other public buildings clustered at the foot of the Mönchsberg – the "Monks' Mountain" – in the narrow strip of land between the cliff and the river. That's the heart of old Salzburg.

A big name in Salzburg was Wolf Dietrich who became Archbishop in 1587, at age 28. His dream was to make Salzburg the Rome of the North. He laid the initial plans for a rebuilt cathedral modelled on St. Peter's, with an adjoining palace on Residenz Square. His splendid Court Stables are now part of the Salzburg Festival complex. Wolf Dietrich and his 17th-century successors changed the face of Salzburg.

Across the river, another steep hill called the Kapuzinerberg dominates the newer side of Salzburg, revolving especially around the early 17th-century Schloss Mirabell and its Garden.

All the sites, each side of the river, are within easy walking distance. The standard city sightseeing tour – normally starting from Mirabell Square – will show you the basic locations, including a trip out to Hellbrunn Castle.

Buildings and Monuments

NOTE: Entry times and prices are for guidance, and may change. Most entrance fees are greatly reduced for children, students and senior citizens.

Hohensalzburg Fortress

Built over the centuries on an ancient Celtic and Roman site, this is now the largest fully preserved medieval castle in Europe. The present castle dates from 1077, with major enlargements around 1500 completed in 1681.

Take the funicular up to the castle, which offers superb views over the city. You can just wander round the fortifications for admission fee of AS 20 or visit the Fortress Museum with a guide for an extra AS 20. Conducted tours can include a Sound and Vision Show, the Fortress Museum and the Rainer Museum, with displays of weaponry and instruments of torture, mainly from 13th to 15th century.

Nonnberg Benedictine Convent

Close to the Fortress is the Convent founded 696 AD, when St. Rupert revived a monastic community which led to the medieval expansion of Salzburg. See the late-Gothic basilica with crypt, 12th-century frescoes, and St. John's Chapel with altar dated 1498.

Cathedral

Located directly below the Fortress, on Domplatz, the Cathedral is the finest early Baroque building north of the Alps and the third to stand on the site. The original building founded 778 by St. Virgil (who was an Irish bishop named O'Farrell) was replaced by a late Romanesque edifice which in turn was destroyed by fire in 1598. The current cathedral was completed in 1628.

The dome was destroyed during World War II but was restored by 1949. The cathedral has a magnificent marble facade, three massive bronze doors (modern, depicting Faith, Hope and Love), a Baroque organ and a Gothic font from 1321. A museum and some excavations are open to the public. Organ recitals are usually given Wed and Sat 11.15 a.m. The Festival performance of "Everyman" – life and death of the rich man – is staged on the Cathedral Square.

Residenz-Platz

Behind the Cathedral leads into Residentz-Platz, distinguished by the largest (40 feet high) baroque fountain outside of Italy, dated 1661. Along one side of the square, adjoining the Cathedral, is the huge **Residenz** – town house of the Prince Bishops – founded 1120, rebuilt 1619, and now used mainly for expositions and classical concerts. The State Rooms are open daily, admission AS 30, with 40-minute conducted tours mostly every 20 minutes from 10 till 16.40 hrs in July and August; at about hourly intervals September till June.

The **Residenz Gallery** features 200 paintings of 16th to 19th centuries – Dutch, French, Italian, and Austrian Baroque. Open 10-17 hrs. Admission AS 30. A combined ticket for State Rooms and Gallery costs AS 40.

Opposite on the square is the **Glockenspiel Tower** rising above the **Residenz New Building**, dating from 1602, which now houses the Central Post Office and departments of the Provincial government. The 35-bell carillon plays tunes by Haydn, Weber and Mozart at 7, 11 and 18 hrs. The chimes can be clearly heard in Residenz Platz. But from November till mid-March on weekdays you can also climb the tower at 10.45 or 17.45 hrs – entry at Mozartplatz 1; fee AS 20.

Mozart Square

Residenz Platz leads into Mozart Square, a lively tourist location containing a central statue of Mozart, erected in 1842. The very clued-up Salzburg Information Office is next door to American Express.

The Shopping Streets

All this area is pedestrianized, and window-shoppers can enjoy walking back beside the Residenz, through the beautiful Alte Markt (Old Market Square) and along Judengasse (formerly part of a ghetto) to Getreidegasse. That richly picturesque cobbled street is famous for dozens of wrought-iron shop signs – many painted or gilded – which hang over the narrow street, giving myriad chances of good photos. In summer, the best time for pictures is around 5 p.m., when afternoon sunshine lights up both sides of the street. Otherwise, Getreidegasse is in shadow most of the day.

Mozart Museum

Look out for the sausage shop at No. 9 Getreidegasse. Above is Mozart's birthplace, now cherished as a museum. The rooms contain a fascinating collection relating to the composer, including his clavichord and first violin, and models of early stage sets from several Mozart operas.

Open daily 9-18 hrs; or till 19 hrs May-Oct. Admission AS 50. Combined tickets for Mozart's Birthplace and Residence (see below) cost AS 70.

Café Winkler

The far end of Getreidegasse leads towards the Mönchsberg lift at Gstättengasse 13 – the energy-saving route to the Café Winkler terrace which offers the finest overall view of Salzburg. Otherwise, turn back to Sigmundsplatz.

Horse-pond and Festival Theatres

On Sigmundsplatz is the astonishing trough built in 1695 for the Prince-Archbishops' 130 horses. Lively frescoes and statues in this monumental construction mask a former quarry.

Next door was the court riding school and stable, which now form part of the Festspielhaus complex where major works are performed during the annual Festival. Outside the July–August period, one or two conducted tours are made of the Festival Halls and Theatre, daily except Sunday, at either 11 or 15 hrs. Fee: AS 30.

Franciscan Church

Past the Festspielhaus and towards the Cathedral is the Franziskanerkirche, founded 1221 with a Romanesque nave, 15th-century Gothic choir, 17th-century side chapels and a baroque High Altar from 1711.

St. Peter's Churchyard

Next comes the Monastery of St. Peter – the oldest surviving monastery in German-speaking lands, founded late 7th century but with a community established even in mid-5th century. Backing onto the sheer rock face of the Mönchsberg is a remarkable cemetery packed with historic tombs of leading Salzburg families. Catacombs can be visited, with 20-minute tours at hourly intervals.

Mozart's Residence, Makartplatz 8

Cross the river on the footbridge called Makartsteg, which leads direct to Markartplatz where the Mozart family lived from 1773 to 1787 while he wrote over 150 works. The house was badly hit in World War II air-raids. All that remains of the original building are the entrance and the "Tanzmeister Saal" which is now a museum devoted to Mozart's life and work during the years 1773–1780.

The museum is open daily in summer (June-Sept) 10-17 hrs. October to May, open daily except Sunday, 10-16 hrs. Entrance AS 35.

Filling the end of the square is the Church of the Holy Trinity, a masterpiece built in 1699 by the Viennese architect Fischer von Erlach, the genius of Austrian baroque. Frescoes are by Michael Rottmayr, who also worked with Erlach on St. Charles' Church in Vienna.

Mozarteum

To complete the Mozart pilgrimage, go back to the Landestheater – Provincial Theatre – on the corner of Schwarzstrasse. Next door is the Marionette Theatre, which includes five Mozart operas in its puppet repertoire.

Then comes the Mozarteum, an Academy of Music – home of the International Mozarteum Foundation – which also operates summer courses. Occasional orchestral concerts are held in the main hall, which rates among the world's finest. In the bastion garden behind the Mozarteum is set a little summer-house originally from Vienna, where Mozart composed *The Magic Flute* in 1791. Visits only during July-August.

Schloss Mirabell and Garden

Next to Makartplatz is the garden of Mirabell Palace, built around 1610 by Archbishop Wolf Dietrich for his Jewish mistress and their twelve children. The grounds and Greek-mythology statues were later designed by Fischer von Erlach, to include an open-air theatre and a Bastion Garden which afterwards was populated with stone dwarves. During the height of summer, young people dibble their feet in the Pegasus fountain. A superb view looks across to the backdrop of Salzburg Castle.

Much rebuilt, the palace is now the Mayor's official residence, while the Marble Room is used for concerts and weddings. The ceremonial Angel Staircase is decorated not with angels but cupids.

Within the complex is a Baroque Museum, open Tue-Sat 9-12 and 14-17 hrs; Sun 9-12 hrs. Entrance AS 30.

Outside, on Mirabell Platz, is departure point for sightseeing tours.

Hellbrunn Palace

From Mirabell Platz bus no. 55 goes direct to Hellbrunn Palace – across the river, along Rudolfskai and thence along Alpenstrasse. This early baroque country retreat was built 1612–1615 for Markus Sittikus, who succeeded his uncle Wolf Dietrich as Prince-Archbishop. Markus Sittikus had somewhat worldly pleasures for a bishop. Judging by the statuary, his favourite god was Bacchus. His fun came from drenching elegant guests with trick fountains, which still operate very effectively. Also worth seeing are the Stone Theatre where the first Italian operas were performed north of the Alps, and the one-month castle – built in record time, and now housing the Salzburg Folklore Museum.

Open Easter to October, 9-17 hrs. Entrance is free to the Park, Orangery and Pheasant Reserve; AS 42 for the Palace, Trick Fountains and Folklore Museum.

3.5 *Other sights in Salzburg*

St Sebastian's Cemetery, Linzergasse 43

Commissioned by Wolf Dietrich in the manner of an Italian "campo santo", it contains the Prince-Archbishop's mausoleum – a magnificent tiled chapel dedicated to Archangel Gabriel. Here also are tombs of the Mozart and Weber families, including Mozart's father Leopold, Mozart's wife Constanze, and her second husband Nikolaus von Nissen.

Kapuzinerberg

To reach one of Salzburg's best viewpoints, start from Linzergasse, through the archway at No. 14. It's a very steep climb past carved Stations of the Cross to the Kapuziner Church on the hilltop. The monastery church is very simply furnished. Its gothic main door dates from mid-15th century, with carved heads of prophets. Further up, a nature reserve is full of splendid lime and chestnut trees, a statue of Mozart and the sound of birds.

Otherwise, keep right of the church, and follow hikers' path no. 804. A little left turning points to "Stadtsaussicht – Hettwer-Bastei". From this bastion you get superb panoramic views of the Old Town. Afterwards, steps lead down Imberg Stiege to Steingasse and thence to the river bank.

Museum of Natural History, Haus der Natur, Museumplatz 5

A very large exhibition of natural history, with an audiovisual show. Open daily 9-17 hrs, entrance AS 35.

Max Reinhard Memorial and Research Centre

Schloss Arenberg, Arenbergstrasse 10

This wonderful museum and study centre is dedicated to the great theatre director Max Reinhard, who founded the

Salzburg Festival. Open: Mon-Fri 9-12 hrs daily. During the Festival open daily 10-12 and 14-17 hrs. Entrance: AS 30.

Salzburg Museum, Museumplatz 1
Dedicated to history of Salzburg. Open: daily except Monday, 9-17 hrs. Entrance: AS 30.

Toy Museum "Bürgerspital", Bürgerspitalplatz 2
A fascinating collection of old toys, applied art and musical instruments. Open: Tue-Sun 9-17 hrs. Entrance AS 25.

National Costume Museum, Griesgasse 23/1
Traditional Salzburg costume, past and present. Open: Mon-Fri 10-12 and 14-17 hrs; Sat 10-12 hrs. Entrance AS 30.

3.6 Take a Trip

On a brief City Break to Salzburg, try to schedule at least one afternoon to enjoy the city's supremely beautiful mountain setting. The wooded hills of Heuberg, Gaisburg and Untersberg are easily accessible by public transport, while the Salzkammergut region of lakes and mountains can best be sampled by coach tour. On a longer stay, add a trip into Germany – to Berchtesgaden where Hitler perched in his "Eagle's Nest".

There are two variations of Salzkammergut circuit. Very popular is the **Sound of Music** tour which combines some Salzburg sightseeing with two lakes – Fuschlsee and Mondsee – and the surrounding hills. The itinerary follows locations where the 1962 movie was filmed, and where the real-life Trapp family played out their personal story.

The regular **Salzkammergut Lakes and Mountains** tour features Lake Wolfgang, with time to explore the resort of St. Wolfgang, where the leading lakeside hotel was model for the operetta *White Horse Inn*. This tour overlaps with the Sound of Music circuit, by stopping at the Collegiate Church in Mondsee, where the wedding scenes were filmed.

3.7 Sunday in Salzburg

There are regular services in the 38 Catholic churches of Salzburg. High Mass is both a religious and a musical experience – orchestra and choir 8.45 a.m. at the Franciscan Church; or with the splendid 4,000-pipe organ at 10 a.m. in the Cathedral. Listen to the greatest works of sacred music, performed in the original setting for which they were composed.

There is only one Protestant church – facing Mirabell Garden at Schwarzstrasse.

All shops are closed Sundays, but most museums and

restaurants are open, and sightseeing excursions are in full operation. There's always choice of musical events, morning, afternoon and evening. Mid-May till mid-August, for instance, there's an open-air promenade concert every Sunday in the Mirabell Garden 10.30-11.30 hrs.

3.8 Shopping

Salzburg is a treasure-trove of high quality, traditional and often hand-made goods. Confectionery, Austrian glassware, petit-point handbags, candles and leather goods are typical products worth investigating.

Shop hours are Monday-Friday 8-18 hrs; Saturday 8-12 or 8-13 hrs. Many shops close for one or two hours at lunch. During the Festival many central shops stay open Saturday afternoon.

The most interesting shopping streets are in the heart of the old city – especially Getreidegasse, Judengasse and Griesgasse. Mainly they sell traditional items, clothes, chocolate, records and books. Across the river around Linzergasse shops tend to be more modern and cheaper, particularly the boutiques.

There's a good open-air market called Schrannenmarkt on Thursday mornings outside St. Andrew's Church on Mirabell Platz – fruit, flowers and veg; leather goods and handicrafts.

A fruit and veg Green Market on Universitäts Platz is open Monday to Friday 6-19 hrs. It's worth a special visit on Saturdays till 13 hrs, when country folk from the Salzkammergut sell all kinds of home-made cakes, cheeses and other products. Fix yourself a stand-up lunch!

3.9 Eating out in Salzburg

Buy a Packed Lunch

Almost every supermarket and delicatessen can make up a 'Semmel' (bread roll) with the meat or cheese of your choice. Depending on the filling, reckon around AS 15. In fine weather it's delightful to picnic by the river or in Mirabell Gardens.

Restaurants for lunch

Sternbräu, Griesgasse 23 – easily reached from Getreidegasse. A complex of restaurants. During summer months there's buffet-style service in the garden courtyard. Relaxed atmosphere with good food at reasonable prices. Open daily 8-24 hrs. Evening music on Fridays and Sundays.

Nordsee, Getreidegasse 27
Excellent seafood dishes and sandwiches to eat-in or take-away. Open 9-19 hrs; from June 1 till Sep 15, open till 23 hrs.

Shrimps Bar, Steingasse 5
Small, relaxed bar with tables outside on the cobbled Steingasse. Wide selection of seafood dishes. Open 11-23 hrs. Closed for two weeks' holiday in July.

McDonald's, on Getreidegasse
Although many people shudder at the idea, McDonald's can be ideal for a quick and cheap lunchtime snack. Open 9 hrs till around midnight.

Maria Plain, Maria Plain Kasern   Tel: 50701
Old mill situated next to a Pilgrimage church, on a hillside outside the city. Can be reached by bus or a no. 77 Lokalbahn from the Bahnhof, and a 20-minute country walk with a great panorama of the surrounding mountains of Salzburg, and of the city itself. Very good Austrian food, featuring local specialities. Closed Wednesdays.

Several **Chinese restaurants** offer set lunches at around AS 60.

For evening dining
Some time during your stay, try the well-known local speciality called Salzburger Nockerl – a super-light soufflé, very sweet. Order it early in the meal, as it takes half an hour to prepare. It arrives looking like three Salzburger mountain peaks, coloured yellow. A serving is plenty for two or three people. See chapter 1.2 for a listing of other Austrian specialities.

Stieglbräu, Rainerstrasse 14   Tel: 77692
Hotel and restaurant belonging to the K&K chain. Has a large beer garden, with very good food and service.

K + K, Waagplatz 2 (just off Mozartplatz)   Tel: 842156
Is slightly more expensive.

Priesterhausstube, Priesterhausgasse 12   Tel: 78317
Small and friendly with traditional decor. Excellent food and service, with big selection of Austrian and international dishes. Try the garlic snails! Open daily except Monday, 17-01 hrs. Reservation advisable.

Zum fidelen Affen, Priesterhausgasse 8   Tel: 77361
Has been described as 'The Drunken Monkey', with a laid-back atmosphere. Popular with the locals, it's a place which one could visit alone and be guaranteed to feel welcome. Austrian food. Open 17-24 hrs, closed Sundays and throughout July.

Wienerwald, Griesgasse 31   Tel: 33375
Very good value, specialising in chicken dishes. Open 7-24 hrs.

Kobenzl, Gaisberg   Tel: 21776
For a very special occasion only! This restaurant is in the

most fantastic position – high above Salzburg with breath-taking views. You'll need taxis each way, adding to the high-cost meal. Reservations usually necessary. Closed Nov-Mar.

Schloss Mönchstein, Mönchsberg 26   Tel: 8413630
An outstanding restaurant for a most special occasion, in a stunning location next to Café Winkler. In this converted castle you get very personal attention, and pay accordingly. Formal dress. Reservation essential, as they have only about six tables. Nouvelle Cuisine.

Hagenauer Stuben, Universitätsplatz 14

Tel: 842657
A cosy candlelit restaurant with excellent Austrian food and wine. In summer you can eat outdoors next to a picturesque market. Let your meal settle by wandering around the art exhibition on the upper floor, which usually features local contemporary artists. Closed Saturday afternoons and Sundays.

Pitter Keller, Rainerstrasse 6-8   Tel: 78571
Renowned for good value. Offers some vegetarian choice including a pasta dish called Spätzle. Also specialises in local cuisine, and has a coffee house and garden. Close to Mirabell Platz, Pitter Keller is handy for lunch, before departure on an afternoon coach tour. Attractive frescoes make it more like a Bavarian Bierkeller, with an evening accordion player to perform April till October.

Zum Mohren, Judengasse 9   Tel: 842387
Historic building, very good Austrian and international cuisine. Reservations advised. Closed Sundays and all through November.

Bärenwirt, Müllner-Haupstrasse 8   Tel: 30386
Located about ten minutes' walk from the main tourist streets. Traditional Austrian food and some vegetarian dishes in friendly surroundings. Open 10 hrs till midnight. Closed Wednesday, except in June till September.

Wilder Mann, on Getreidegasse   Tel: 841787
In a small courtyard, has lots of character, and is frequented especially by locals. Large portions. They do a good Salzburger Nockerl.

Stiftskeller St. Peter, St. Peterbezirk 1   Tel: 841268
Claims to be Austria's oldest restaurant, dating from 803. Hot and cold snacks or a full meal in a medieval atmosphere, with outdoor eating and drinking at benches and tables in the courtyard, or beneath the hollowed-out cliff. Handily located below the Festung for people who have been to a concert. Closed Mondays.

A short-list of cafés

There are dozens of charming cafés all over Salzburg. But here are a few favourites which are worth a special visit.

Tomaselli, Alter Markt 9
Traditional decor. Usually crowded with a good atmosphere. It was founded in 1703 by an Italian singer at the court. He married a girl whose father had the original license to serve coffee. Tomaselli gave up singing, and opened the coffeeshop which is still operated by the same family. When Mozart's wife was widowed, she then married a Danish diplomat who wrote the definitive biography of Mozart. They lived on the floor above the café.

Café Glockenspiel
Very large, taking up an entire side of Mozart Square. It's a good base for watching the tourist world go by, and for listening to the Carillon at 11 a.m. or 6 p.m.

Bazar, Schwarzstrasse 3
An institution for the locals – everyone goes! Atmosphere in abundance. Its riverside terrace offers a delightful view across the Salzach. Closed Sundays.

Café Winkler – reached by lift up the Mönchsberg – is very nice for a refreshment. Expensive, but you're also paying for the view.

Hotel Stein, by the Stadtsbrücke
During July and August, Hotel Stein opens a rooftop café with a fantastic view over the inner city.

3.10 Nightlife

Salzburg delights music-lovers not only during its world-famed summer Festival. Concerts, theatre and folk events are never out of season, and it's usually possible to get tickets *somewhere*. Around 15 official agencies sell tickets to all the main events at a standard 20% mark-up. Outside the big Festival season, programmes are mainly of chamber music. One of the pleasures is to hear these concerts in their original settings – not in a modern hall, but in the princely rooms where the performances were first given. Price-guide: AS 250.

Best policy is to pick up the month's programme, published by the Salzburg Tourist Office, and go direct to the concert or theatre box office. As Salzburg is so small, it's really quite easy to drop by on your sightseeing rounds, and save the mark-up.

But don't just turn up on the night! Auditoriums are small, and all seats are normally filled. Try for the Salzburg Palace Concerts, which are held either at **Mirabell Palace** or at the **Residenz** next to the Cathedral. Similar performances are given at the **Festung**, where concerts are held in the splendid Fürstenzimmer from May till October. Seats are unnumbered. So, if you don't want a back seat, arrive half an hour early, when the doors open.

Other historic concert venues include the **Gothic Hall** of St. Blasius Church at the end of Getreidegasse, the **Mozarteum** on Schwarzstrasse, and out at **Hellbrunn Castle** for Mozart Serenades. Price range is AS 150-350.

Outside the Salzburg Festival season, live opera is infrequent except for some performances between mid-September and the first week of June at the **Landestheater**, close to the Mozarteum on Schwarzstrasse. Otherwise, for frustrated opera-lovers, a light-hearted alternative is offered by the **Marionetten Theater** next door.

To the recorded music of past Festival opera performances, life-size puppets perform in realistic style. The current repertoire of nine operas and operettas includes five works by Mozart. The marionettes' main Salzburg season runs April through September, including matinees during the Festival. They then rest for a month before departing on foreign tours. Prices are 250-350 AS.

Salzburg Festival

For a dedicated music-lover, the Salzburg Festival is the dream of a lifetime. During the five-week season in July/August, the repertoire always includes at least six operas among the overall total of 130 performances in the full programme.

Ticket-buying demands advance planning! Especially for the big events, don't expect just to pick up tickets on arrival – though sometimes your friendly hotel concierge can oblige if you can face a huge mark-up. To buy tickets at cost price, here's the drill:

At the beginning of December, the Festival programme is published. Send for a copy from the ticket office in Salzburg – Kartenbüro der Salzburger Festspiele, Festspielhaus, A-5010 Salzburg. The programme contains an order form, for sending to the ticket office before the deadline of around January 7. By the end of March, they will advise what tickets can be allocated. Then you must immediately settle the account, so that tickets can be despatched by registered post.

If you miss that priority chance, just write later to the ticket office, in the hope of any seats left over from the first orders, or from cancellations.

The last chance is on-the-spot – first at the Festival box office, which is open Mon-Fri 9.30-17.00 hrs. There's also a ticket office called Polzer on Residenz Platz, next to the Cathedral, which handles returned tickets and cancellations.

If no luck, then go from one ticket agency to another. You may not get the seat or the performance of your dreams. But if you just want to participate in the Salzburg Festival – and every performance is superlative – then there's always chance of getting *something*. Opera ticket prices start at 500 AS, and reach 3,000 AS. For concerts, reckon a range of 150-1000 AS. Dress is formal. For prime occasions, such as Festival premieres, tails or dinner jacket; evening gown.

On the lighter side

Salzburg is not a city which explodes at night-time. It can be very quiet. Many visitors expect some Tyrolean-type oompah bands in restaurants. But that's not the Salzburg style, except for Wednesday evening folklore evenings during summer months at the **Stiegel-Keller** at Festungs-gasse 10, just below the fortress. Folk-music and dance performances are also given in the **Fortress Restaurant** – Tuesday and Friday, June till late September.

For younger people, there are many good bars – tucked away, quite discreet. Bars along Giselakai are always popular, and clubs can be found off Neumayrplatz. For something different try the **Felsenkeller**, at Toscanini Hof by the Festspielhaus. Until midnight you can enjoy wine in a coin-studded cellar built right into the cliff.

Salburg Casino operates daily from 3 p.m. till the small hours at Café Winkler on Mönchsberg – French and American roulette, blackjack, one-arm bandits, and baccarat at weekends. They give you a starter kit of chips worth AS 200 for cut-price AS 170, and you also ride free on the lift. Take passport!

3.11 At your service

(See also section 2-11 for information applicable to both Salzburg and Vienna – Phone Calls, News, Medical, Tipping.)

Money and Banking

Bank hours are Monday-Friday 8-12 and 14-16.30 hrs. Exchange Bureau at Main Railway Station – Daily 7-22 hrs. Bankhaus Daghofer at Griesgasse 11 is also open Sat 8.30-17 hrs, and Sun 9-16 hrs.
Rieger Bank, Judengasse 13 is also open Sat 9.30-14 hrs, and on Sundays during the Festival 10-15 hrs.
In July/August, exchange offices are likewise open Sat and Sun at the Tourist Information Centre in Mozart Square, and at the Fortress funicular exchange office. The exchange office at Alter Markt opens Sat 9.30-12 hrs July to September.

Post and Telephone

Main Post Office with Poste Restante service:
Residenzplatz 9. Open: Mon-Fri 7-19 hrs; Sat 8-10 hrs. Closed: Sundays.

Calls to UK: see information in Vienna chapter, Section 2.11

Emergency phone numbers

Police	133
Fire	122
Ambulance	144
Doctor or Dentist, Information:	71327 or 71328

Should you have anything stolen, you must report it to the Police for insurance purposes, whereupon you will be issued with a declaration.
Police Headquarters and Lost Property Office (Mon-Fri 7-12.30 hrs) Alpenstrasse 90   29511

Medical

For information on the nearest general practitioner, specialist or dentist:
Ärztekammer für Salzburg, Schrannengasse 2
Tel: 71327/8
Emergency Centre, Paris-Lodron-Strasse 8a   Tel: 141
Open: Sat 7 a.m. till Mon 7.a.m. and public holidays
Pharmaceutical Chemists
General Opening: Mon-Fri 8-12 and 14.30-18 hrs; Sat 8-12 hrs.
Night and Sunday service: If closed, shops display a list of nearest night chemist.
Hospitals
Accident Hospital: Dr Franz-Rehrl-Platz 5
Tel: 725210
Hospital of the Barmherzigen Brüder, Kajetanerplatz 1
Tel: 844531
Dentists
Österreicher Dentistenkammer, Gstättengasse
Tel: 843777

Consulates

UK, Alter Markt 4	Tel: 848133
USA, Giselakai 51	Tel: 28601

Salzburg Tourist Office

For information, maps or brochures on Salzburg or the surrounding area, contact the very helpful Tourist Office at Mozartplatz 5   Tel: 847568
There's also an Information Office at the Railway Station on Platform 10   Tel: 71712
HQ of the City Tourist Office (Stadtverkehrsbüro) is at Auerspergstrasse 7   Tel: 80720

Chapter Four

Budapest

4.1. Introduction to Budapest

For the best panorama of Budapest, stand on Gellert Hill – a rock that rises steeply, 430 feet above the river bank. Down below is the Danube, almost 1,000 yards wide. The river splits the Hungarian capital into two sections: the hills of Buda on the right bank; the plain of Pest on the left.

The Buda hills formed the original settlement: Castle Hill, with a fortress and Royal Palace, the ancient Matthias Church where Hungarian kings were crowned for 600 years, and the more modern Fishermen's Bastion which is another fine viewing point.

All around on Castle Hill are delightful old streets of medieval, baroque and classical houses. This is the romantic old-time Budapest that flourished when Budapest was part of the Austro–Hungarian Empire.

Across the Danube bridges lies the Inner City, called Belvaros – the heart of old Pest, which originally was independent of Buda.

Within that Inner City it's mainly an 18th- and 19th-century world of baroque churches, turn-of-the-century shops, cafés and restaurants, and a ministerial and political nucleus that focuses around the neo-gothic Parliament House that looks like a riverside copy of London's Parliament without Big Ben.

Further up-stream, the River Danube splits into two arms that form Margaret Island – 200 acres of public park used as a major sport and recreation centre. Like a complete resort, it has tennis courts, swimming pools with artificial waves, amusement centres, rose-gardens, open-air theatres, cafés, restaurants and a Grand Hotel.

And all around is the Danube, with paddle-steamers, hydrofoils and launches that offer a variety of river trips, some with meals, music and dancing.

On Margaret Island you can sample a bathing-pool of hot sulphur water, fed by one of Budapest's 123 thermal springs – a big share of the 400 mineral springs that exist in Hungary as a whole. The Romans fell in love with Budapest because of the hot baths, and visitors have been taking the waters ever since. At the bottom of Gellert Hill is a large spa hotel with thermal baths, swimming pools

and other spa amenities, including an orchestra with your meals.

Budapest ranks as Eastern Europe's liveliest capital, having made an early break from the heavy Moscow style. The process has accelerated, with dumping of red stars, much faster moves towards a market economy, opening of a Stock Exchange, and renaming of streets that had been dedicated to the former ideology. Local maps and all guide-books find it hard to keep pace!

Budapest is a musical city. Gipsy bands are everywhere: in hotels at teatime, to accompany coffee and cake; in speciality restaurants; in wine-cellars that stay open till past midnight; on Danube steamers that offer evening cruises.

Often the musicians are dressed in formal evening suits with black bow-ties; otherwise they are brightly clad in traditional costume, all ready to smile at the flashguns. Their gipsy music is enchanting, switching from mood to mood through an evening of Magyar nostalgia.

On a more serious note, Budapest can offer the widest possible choice of classical music, year-round.

In summer the main attraction of Budapest is sightseeing: the scenery, the Danube and excursions to Lake Balaton. In winter, visitors come especially for the mental refreshment of cultural events, with the added attraction that off-season hotel prices are much lower. But always there's great pleasure in sampling the rich variety of Hungarian cuisine, supported by the excellent Hungarian wines. A few days in Budapest can be a very memorable experience.

4.2 Arrival & hotel

Visas for UK passport holders were abolished in October 1990, as part of the liberalization process. By air, London Heathrow to Budapest is served daily by either British Airways or Malév. There are daily flights from Vienna by Malév or Austrian Airlines. By train from Vienna's Westbahnhof takes about 5 hours.

There are two public buses a day from Vienna to Budapest, taking $4\frac{1}{2}$ hours and costing about £13. A more expensive alternative is to travel along the Danube by hydrofoil, to disembark by Elizbeth Bridge (Erzsebet hid).

If you're arriving by air, transfer to your hotel is by bus or taxi, taking about 30 minutes to the centre. An airport bus goes direct to the very central Engels Square. By public transport, take black number 93 bus from airport to Kobanya-Kispest station on blue Metro line 3. By whichever method, the fare is very low.

Hotels follow the standard international grading system of one to five stars. Most of them are very central, mainly on the Pest side of the river within walking distance of the main sights or easily reached in a few minutes by the very frequent and low-cost public transport.

4.3 Getting around Budapest

Public transport offers you wide choice of trams, trolley buses, buses and Metro. There are no conductors. Following the usual Central European honour system, passengers punch their own ticket when they board. Tickets and day passes can be purchased in tobacconist's shops, at tram and bus terminals, at railway stations, and at travel offices.

There are two kinds of ticket. One is valid for use any distance on trams, trolley buses, Metro and the suburban railway (HEV) as far as the city limits. The blue bus ticket costs slightly more.

Stopping places show frequency of service, and times of the first and last vehicles. An unbroken line displays the route and a small arrow indicates the stop where you're standing. Smoking or use of portable radios is not allowed on public transport vehicles.

Trams

There are 38 tram routes on a very frequent schedule from 4 a.m. till midnight. A few main lines operate all night. A very useful service is 2 and 2A, which shuttles along the Pest river embankment.

Buses

The blue Ikarus buses operate on 208 bus routes. Buses with black numbers stop at every halt on their route. Those with red numbers are express services stopping only at specially indicated halts. Those with letter E after a red number travel non-stop from one terminal to another. Services operate 04.30 till 23.00 hrs, with a few main routes operating all night.

Metro

There are three Metro lines – easy to use, and all meeting at Deak ter. They operate between 4.30 a.m. and 23.10 hrs (till midnight on yellow line).

Number 1, yellow line, runs between Mexikoi ut and Vorosmarty ter.

Number 2, red line, runs between Ors Vezer tere and the Deli Palyaudvar (Southern Railway Station).

Number 3, blue line, operates between Kobanya-Kispest MAV Allomas (railway station) and Arpad-Hid.

The most useful stations for visitors are:

Vorosmarty ter for the heart of the pedestrianized shopping streets along Vaci utca; also closest to the three riverside luxury hotels – Atrium Hyatt, Forum and Duna Inter-Continental.

Deak ter is also very close.

Kossuth ter is nearest to the Parliament building.

Astoria or **Kalvin ter** are handy for the National Museum.

Hosok tere (Heroes' Square) is best for the Fine Art

Museum and for the Agricultural Museum in Vajdahunyad Castle and Varosliget Park.

From **Moskva ter**, a little blue bus labelled Budavari Siklo takes you quickly up the steep hill to the Castle area, with several stops inside the ramparts.

Funicular

A very useful funicular operates from Buda side of the Chain Bridge up to the Royal Palace in Castle District, with splendid views by day or night.

Trolley buses

There are twelve trolley routes, most of which connect with the Metro.

HEV (Suburban Railway)

This service offers connections to villages surrounding the capital. There are four lines: Godollo, Csepel, Rackeve and Szentendre. The Szentendre line is particularly important, serving that beautiful resort village on the Danube (see section 4.6). Its starting point is **Batthyany ter** on Metro red line.

Other transport services include a cogwheel railway, river boats and minibuses.

Taxis

You can order by calling Fotaxi 122-2222 or Volantaxi 166-6666. To reserve a taxi an hour or more in advance dial 118-8888. Cabs are metered in the usual way, but Western vehicles like Mercedes are more expensive than those from Eastern Europe. Generally, if you're watching your funds, don't catch a taxi outside the big hotels. The fare could easily double. Tipping: if the fare is around 100 Ft. give a 20-Ft tip; up to 400 or 500 Ft, make it 10%.

"Ibusz City"

Another way of Budapest sightseeing: tour buses circle every 30 minutes on a fixed itinerary around town, to include all the main locations and sights. Having bought your day's ticket, you can get on or off at any of the 17 stops.

Orientation

Four main bridges link the sightseeing zones of Buda and Pest.

Margaret Bridge – Margit hid – gives access to the mid-Danube park of Margaret Island.

Chain Bridge – Szechenyi lanchid. From Roosevelt Square beside the Atrium Hyatt hotel you can cross to Buda on the Chain Bridge which was built by a British engineer, Adam Clark, in the 1840's. It was the first bridge across the Danube at this point. From Clark Adam Square a major road – also built by Adam Clark – is tunnelled below Castle Hill, while the funicular offers an easy ride to the summit. A circular stone carving near the funicular marks the zero point from which all Hungarian distances from Budapest are measured.

Elizabeth Bridge – Erzsebet hid – is named after Emperor Franz Joseph's wife who was assassinated in 1898. The original chain bridge was demolished by the Germans in 1945, to be replaced by the present suspension bridge in 1964.

Liberty Bridge – Szabadsag hid – leads across from the Central Market area (see section 4.8) to Gellert Hill.

River Port

On the Pest side, between Elizabeth and Liberty Bridge, the river bank serves as an international river port and frontier zone! This is where passport formalities are conducted for passengers aboard international boats such as the hydrofoil service from Vienna.

4.4 Basic Budapest

Here's a short list of Essential Budapest, aimed at capturing the flavour of this lively capital.

(1)   Make the most of the standard City Sightseeing tour, which includes time at magnificent viewpoints like Gellert Hill and the Fishermen's Bastion.

(2)   Spend several hours, daytime or evening, exploring the streets and buildings of Castle Hill.

(3)   Take an evening dinner cruise on the Danube with gipsy music and wild Hungarian folk-dancing.

(4)   Sample rich pastries at Gerbaud's on Vorosmarty Square.

(5)   Shop-gaze along Vaci utca, and look for bargains in folk art, books, records, Herend procelain and Helia-D cosmetics.

(6)   See the Hungarian crown jewels on first floor of the National Museum.

(7)   Enjoy an evening stroll along the Dunakorzo Promenade, now lined with big international hotels.

(8)   Travel to the beautiful Danube Bend by coach or boat, with time to explore Szentendre.

(9)   Wallow in the thermal baths at Hotel Gellert or at Thermal on Margit Island, as reminder of why Roman soldiers enjoyed a posting to this city.

(10) Visit the Central Market Hall near Szabadsag Bridge, for colourful displays of farm products.

A guided sightseeing tour of Budapest is the best introduction to the city. If you haven't already booked, contact your rep for a reservation. The starting point for most coach tours operated by Ibusz is near a very conspicuous Chinese restaurant called Szechuan on Roosevelt Square, which is next to the Atrium Hyatt hotel and facing Chain Bridge.

The two halves of Budapest couldn't be more different. On one side of the Danube ancient Buda rises and falls over seven hills. On the other side, Pest – the government and commercial centre of the capital – is impressive with its grand boulevards, squares and buildings.

The Castle District of Buda

Most visitors return several times to Castle Hill, which offers fascination at every turn: cobbled streets, Baroque mansions and medieval courtyards high above the rest of the city. The entire district was devastated when German Nazi troops held out against the Russian army from December 1944 until mid-February 1945. It took 20 years to complete the restoration, totally in the original harmonious style.

Matthias Church – Matyas templom

The Church of Our Lady with its slender Gothic spire is also known as the Coronation church, where a number of Hungarian kings were crowned. More often it's called Matthias Church, after the 15th-century King Matthias whose coat of arms appears on the south tower.

During Turkish occupation, the building was converted into the city's principal mosque. After the return of Christian forces, it was then rebuilt in Baroque style, followed in the 19th century by yet another reconstruction in neo-Gothic. Within, the cathedral still shows some stylized Islamic decoration – on the columns, for instance – as reminder of the building's 150 years as a mosque.

The church stands on Holy Trinity Square – named after the 18th-century Trinity Statue erected in thanksgiving for deliverance from the plague. The square is focalpoint for private-sector tourism. Here is pick-up point for horse-and-buggy rides. The drivers charge 600 to 1000 Ft for a 15-minute trot around. Buskers and handicraft vendors spill over into the Fishermen's Bastion area, which is thick with instant-portrait artists and currency hustlers.

Fishermen's Bastion – Halasz Bastya

Although this monument could pass as medieval with its turrets, terraces and arches it was actually built early this century. According to tradition this stretch of the medieval ramparts was defended by the fishermen's guild, hence the name. The panorama is magnificent, across the Danube to the Parliament building and right round to Gellert Hill.

Alongside is the Budapest Hilton, which – despite its ultra-modern appearance with copper-glass facade – fits in quite well, and doesn't spoil the view from across the river.

Three parallel side streets lead off from Holy Trinity Square (Szentharomsag ter) and Hess Andras ter – Tancsics

Mihaly utca, Fortuna utca and Orszaghaz utca. Virtually every other building displays a plaque marking it as a historic monument. The beautiful baroque houses and mansions all have medieval foundations. You can easily cover the area in a one-hour stroll. But it's worth spending longer to absorb the atmosphere, perhaps staying for an evening meal and seeing the area under the added glamour of nightfall. Look specially for these highlights:

Tancsics Mihaly utca – In medieval times, this was a Jewish street – no. 26 is the Jewish Oratory with relics excavated from that time. The street is named after the revolutionary writer who was imprisoned at no. 9 with Lajos Kossuth in 1848. Previously that building housed the Royal Mint. Next door, no. 7, was formerly the Erdody Palace where Beethoven stayed in 1800. It's now the **Museum of Music History**, with musical instruments displayed in the workshop of Bela Bartok. (Open Wed-Sun 10-18 hrs; Mon 16-21 hrs; closed Tue.)

Fortuna utca – At no. 4 is the **Museum of Commerce and Catering** which displays everything from old menus to kitchen utensils and the confectionery business. The commerce section covers history of trade in the first half of the 20th century. The building itself was previously the Fortuna Inn.

Orszaghaz utca (Parliament Street) – Look particularly at nos. 18, 20 and 22, which were built in 14th and 15th centuries and give an idea of how the Castle District looked in medieval times. During Turkish occupation, several baths – hamams – were located along this street.

At the far end of these three streets is the Esztergom Bastion which completes the castle ramparts, with an exit called Vienna Gate – walk up for yet another viewpoint. The **Museum of Military History** on Toth Arpad Promenade covers the history of hand weapons, knights from the time of King Matthias, the Revolution and War of Independence of 1848-49; World War 1, and the Hungarian army from 1920 to the present. (Open: daily except Mon, 9-18 hrs.)

Back to Trinity Square, Tarnok utca or Uri utca both lead towards the upper end of the cable car from Chain Bridge, and to the Royal Palace. Along those two streets are some more beautifully reconstructed houses. Several embassies are located in this area. At Uri utca 9 is entrance to some damp Catacombs and a Waxwork Exhibition.

Buda Castle Palace

The Palace you see today originally developed from a modest 13th century construction. As different monarchs came to power each wanted to impress their countrymen with an even more splendid Palace. The neo-Baroque building today evolved during reconstruction in the 19th and 20th centuries. It has been completely rebuilt since the siege of 1945 when it was used by the Germans as a command post. From the parapet you can see how the palace-castle totally dominated the river crossing.

As the largest public building in Budapest, the Palace now houses three museums – National Gallery, Budapest History Museum and the National Library. The **National Gallery** has the most interest for visitors, featuring Hungarian art from 14th century onwards, but specially rich in evocative late 19th-century painting.

At the front entrance to the Royal Palace, overlooking the Danube, is a statue of Prince Eugene of Savoy, the Austrian general who ejected the Turks from their 150 years' occupation of the city.

Gellert Hill

Another style of Liberation Monument rears dramatically 45 feet high on top of Gellert Hill, and is visible from all parts of the city. A Soviet war memorial with the statue of a woman holding a palm leaf of freedom is symbolic of liberation from Nazi rule, and was erected in 1947. Behind the monument is the Citadel – a fortress built in mid-19th century by the Austrians, after the collapse of the Hungarian War of Independence. Within the once-menacing walls are a restaurant, café and hotel.

Gellert Hill is named after the Italian missionary Bishop Ghirardus (Gellert), who converted the country to Christianity. He died a martyr's death in 1046, when pagan Hungarians nailed him into a barrel and rolled him off the clifftop. His personal monument faces Elizabeth Bridge, along the steep route down to the river.

Rudas Baths (Rudas furdo)

At the bottom of Gellert Hill, close to Elizabeth Bridge, are the men-only Rudas thermal baths, built by the Turks in 1556. Although the building has been altered substantially over the years a splendid Turkish dome still rises over one octagonal pool. When the sun shines through, it creates dramatic effects.

Also below the Hill, by Szabadsag Bridge, is the famous Gellert Hotel and Baths, built 1913 to offer spa treatment.

Belvaros – the Inner City

During medieval times, while Buda's Castle Hill was settled by people dependent on the palaces and forts, the east bank was the tradesmen's end: a quite separate town called Pest (pronounced 'Pesht'). A city wall marked the boundary, which is followed today by the so-called Kiskorut (Little Boulevard) – from Liberty Bridge to Chain Bridge via Muzeum korut, Tanacs korut, Jozsef Attila utca and Roosevelt Square – with the curving river bank to form a lemon-shaped area of tightly-packed 19th-century building.

Vorosmarty ter and Vaci utca

One of Pest's main centres is the square called Vorosmarty ter, named after a 19th-century patriotic poet whose statue stands in the middle. In summertime dozens of artists offer an on-the-spot portrait service, with entertainers to supply background music. This square leads into the cosmopolitan Vaci utca, which runs parallel to the Danube, behind the big international hotels. Together with the side streets, and up to Deak square, it all makes a very pleasant pedestrian precinct. Day and night it's a lively area, with some of the best shops, boutiques, cafés and restaurants of Budapest.

Dunakorzo – the Danube Promenade

Stroll along the Danube waterfront for the glorious panorama of the Buda Hills across the river. Three large international hotels – Atrium Hyatt, Forum and Duna Inter-Continental – have given a new postwar look to the promenade, which was a prewar favourite for a leisured stroll.

Vigado Square is embarkation point for pleasure cruises – a wide range of choices, some with meals and music. The square takes its name from the Vigado Concert Hall dating from 1865. Besides its large concert hall, the building includes a small theatre, restaurant and a magnificent staircase.

Parliament – Orsaghaz

Facing the Chain Bridge is Roosevelt Square. Continue further along the embankment to reach Kossuth Lajos Square and the Parliament building. In a mixture of Renaissance and Gothic, the building was originally constructed to reflect the grandeur of the Austro–Hungarian Empire. In style and riverside location it greatly resembles London's Houses of Parliament.

Facing Parliament is the Ministry of Agriculture and then another look-alike: the **Ethnographic Museum**, which could double for the Berlin Reichstag. This neo-Renaissance palace was built in the 1890's and now houses collections from ancient times to modern days.

On the square between these buildings is a statue of Kossuth Lajos, who was a leader of the Hungarian Independence movement of 1848. Crucial political demonstrations have swirled around his statue. Elsewhere on the square – among trees by the embankment – is a dreamy statue of Atilla Jozsef, a poet who lived 1905 to 1937. Especially he is known for his poem about sitting beside the river, just watching the water float by. Maybe that's an even better way of enjoying Basic Budapest.

4.5 Other sights in Budapest

Museums and art galleries

Unless otherwise noted, museums are open daily except

Mondays from 10-18 or 9-17 hrs. Entrance prices are minimal. At weekends, all museums are free.

National Museum, Muzeum korut 14-16
Looking like a smaller version of the British Museum, this is Hungary's most important collection, and includes history of the Hungarian peoples. Among the Coronation Regalia is the crown of St. Stephen which spent over 30 years in USA, until its return in 1978.

Museum of Fine Arts, Dozsa Gyorgy ut 41, Hosok tere – Heroes' Square
Displays the Egyptian collection, a rich supply of old masters, graphic arts, and modern painting and sculpture. For art lovers, this museum rates very high among Europe's galleries – far richer than most people expect. The collection of Spanish paintings is outstanding.

Museum of Applied Art, IX, Ulloi ut 33-37
Varied art and crafts; and tapestries from late 19th century till World War II.

Aquincum Museum, 111, Szentendrei ut 139
Remains of the Roman city, along the road towards Szentendrei. Open May to October.

Transport Museum, XIV, Varosligeti korut 11
In Varosliget Park – numerous displays, with working models.

Andrassy ut
This grand boulevard has reverted to its former name, after years of being called Nepkoztarsasag utja - Avenue of the People's Republic – and still shown thus, on most city maps. Its style resembles the Champs Elysées in Paris, ending in Heroes' Square for the big State occasions. It reaches from the Inner Boulevard to the City Park. Most of the buildings date from between 1872 and 1885, and have some unique feature such as a fountain or statue in their courtyards.

Buses 1 and 4 run the whole distance, while underground is the century-old Metro line 1 – the oldest in continental Europe. Train buffs should visit the Metro Museum in the Deak Square pedestrian underpass – open Wed-Sun. The principal buildings along the avenue include:

Postal Museum at no. 3 – Relics from Post Office history, telecommunications, and 60 years of radio.

Opera House at no. 22, restored to its original splendour. The associated **Budapest Operetta Theatre** is two streets further along, in Magymezo utca.

Ballet Institute at no. 25.

Hungarian Academy of Music in a square (right) called

Liszt Ferenc ter with a statue of Franz Liszt in the middle. The Academy, built 1904-07 in Art Nouveau style, houses a large concert hall.

Ferenc Liszt Museum at no. 35, the composer's former home. (Open Mon-Fri 10-18 hrs; Sat 9-17 hrs.) A chamber music concert is performed every Sat at 11 a.m.

Academy of Fine Arts at no. 71.

Composer **Zoltan Kodaly**'s former residence at no. 89.

Heroes' Square – Hosok tere
The 47-ton centrepiece to Heroes' Square is the Millenary Monument erected in 1896 to commemorate the 1,000th anniversary of Magyar conquest of the country. There are statues of leading figures in Hungarian history – kings, tribal chiefs and war heroes. Until 1956, postwar visitors viewed a huge Stalin on a vast plinth. But he was chopped up during the opening hours of the Hungarian Revolution in October 1956.

The Museum of Fine Arts (see above) and an Art Gallery Exhibition Hall (looking like a Greek temple) are located each side of the square, with Varosliget – City Park – in the background. Easiest access is direct by Metro line 1 from downtown.

Varosliget – City Park
Right behind Heroes' Square is Budapest's largest park – 250 green acres that include a boating lake which becomes an ice rink in winter. Across the lake, reflected in the waters, is the make-believe **Castle of Vajdahunyad**. Like the monument in Heroes' Square, it was built as part of the millenary celebrations of 1896. The aim was to incorporate every architectural style that had ever been used in Hungary's 1,000-year history. The building is home for an **Agricultural Museum** which covers farming, fishing and hunting. (Open daily except Mon 10-16 hrs.) In the courtyard is a mysterious hooded statue of Anonymous, the unknown Royal Scribe who wrote the first Hungarian chronicles.

The park also houses the triple domed Szechenyi Baths – one of Europe's largest medicinal bath complexes – as well as Gundel's luxury-grade restaurant, the giant beer tent of the Royal Bavarian Brewery, a small zoo and botanical garden, an amusement park for the kids, and the Transport Museum. Altogether it's a good place to see how Hungarians relax.

Margaret Island – Margitsziget
This Danube island is about 1.5 miles long, virtually traffic free and protected from noise by planted plane-trees. It's a favourite spot for a peaceful two-hour stroll. Among the

attractions are swimming complexes, an open-air theatre, open-air cinema, and a thermal water spring with goldfish. Enjoy the tranquil terrace setting of the Ramada Grand Hotel.

Buda Hills

As a change from city sightseeing take the cog wheel train to Liberty Hill. The terminal is opposite Hotel Budapest on Szilagyi Erzsebet fasor – access from Moskva ter on tram no. 18 or bus 56. You travel through greenery, villas and gardens into open spaces where, close to the last stop, you can ride on the **Pioneer Railway**. This is operated by school children dressed in the smart uniforms of station masters, ticket sellers and conductors.

Summer visitors can take the chair-lift (Libego) to the top of Janos Hill where it is possible to see more than 45 miles on a clear day. There's access from Moskva ter on bus no. 158.

4.6 Take a trip

Danube Bend

The prime excursion out of Budapest is upstream to the Danube Bend, where the river narrows and turns sharply as it passes between the 2500-3000 ft heights of the Pilis and the Borzsony Mountains.

This strategic Bend is overlooked by the hilltop fortress-palace of Visegrad – first developed by the Romans, then built up by the Hungarian kings from 13th century onwards. This was the official royal seat in the early Middle Ages – not in Buda. By the 15th century, Visegrad rated high among the great palaces of Central Europe.

Destroyed by the Turks in 1542, the site was forgotten until rediscovered in 1943. Since then, restoration has given Visegrad very high rating as a tourist attraction. There are superb views of the Danube Bend itself, and of controversial preparations for a mammoth hydro-electric complex – now abandoned through popular outcry.

En route to Visegrad is Szentendre – a small and charming riverside town which originally was settled by Greek and Serbian migrants. Szentendre has become a mini resort, with numerous cafés, restaurants and cheerful souvenir shops, boutiques and peasant craftware stalls.

Near Szentendre is the Skanzen: a museum of peasant houses and village buildings which have been transported from different parts of Hungary, re-erected and furnished in authentic style. On certain days young people perform traditional activities, like harvesting and making bread.

Danube Bend excursions are operated by motor coach or river boat. Part of the pleasure comes from admiring the prosperous-looking private homes along the road, each standing in its own large garden, packed with flowers, fruit and vegetables. Many houses offer rooms to let – "Zimmer frei".

Lake Balaton

A popular arrangement is to split summer holiday time between Budapest and Lake Balaton. The 48-mile lake is the largest inland sea of Central Europe, and is well developed for the sunshine business. A splendid landmark is the twin-spired cathedral dominating the Tihany peninsula that almost cuts the lake in half. The lake shores are shallow and offer warm bathing. There are beaches, little yacht harbours, and facilities for water sports and fishing.

But the greatest delight comes from exploring the wine-villages, and tasting vintages. There are photos, everywhere you look. Long single-storeyed farmhouses are thatched and lime-washed. In late summer, blood-red paprikas dry against a sunny wall.

If you can spare another day from your Budapest City Break, put Balaton high on your list of where to go!

4.7 Sunday in Budapest

All shops are closed, but cafés, restaurants, museums, art galleries and sightseeing tours are in full operation.

For High Mass in a superb setting, go to Matthias Church in the Castle District. An orchestra and choir perform classical sacred works every Sunday at 10 a.m.

Inner City Parish Church - Belvarosi Templom

This is the oldest surviving structure in Pest, located on the approach to Elizabeth Bridge. The twin Baroque towers and the facade date from early 19th Century, but the church was founded in 12th Century.

Basilica (St Stephen's Parish Church)

This is the biggest church in Budapest and took from 1851 to 1905 to complete. The church holds 8,000 people, and is often filled to capacity during services.

Sunday Markets

XI Fhervar ut 14. (6-13 hrs)
XIII Elmunkas ter. (6-14 hrs)

4.8 Shopping in Budapest

What to buy?

Food and Drink: browse through the supermarkets for Hungarian salami, paprika spice, golden Tokaj and a bottle of barack apricot brandy. Maybe you have acquired a taste for all four, so what better memento?

Handicrafts: survey the folk-art shops for hand-woven cushion covers, costume dolls, lace and embroidered tablecloths which mostly come from Transylvania. Copper and brass bowls, vases, ashtrays etc make good presents. Look for leather goods, silver, woodwork and precious stones. Carpets and rugs are reasonable priced, even those which are homespun and hand-knotted.

Ceramics: the most famous factory, at Herend near the Austrian border, has been producing porcelain since 1839. Queen Victoria ordered some for Windsor Castle in 1851, and the White House bought Herend ware for state banquets. The hand-painted designs are in rich variety, 19th-century rather than modern: animal pieces galore, floral patterns and Ming-like teapots and pedestal cake stands. Figurines of typical Hungarian characters are also popular.

Books, records and games: there are some excellent books in English, remarkably low-cost. Also worth buying are recordings of Hungarian folk-music, classical CD's and cassettes; and teasers in three-dimensional logic – successors to the Rubik Cube – from the Rubik Studio. There's a Soviet cultural store opposite Astoria Hotel, where you can buy Soviet records and cassettes at very cheap prices.

Finally, a curiosity: many visitors buy bottles of a famous tonic and cure-all called Beres Csepp. This and Banfi hair lotion for thinning hair – said to halt the process – can be found in Herbaria shops.

Shopping areas

The principal shops are along the Great Boulevard formed by the boulevards of Szt Istvan, Lenin, Jozsef and Ferenc; and along Kossuth Lajos Street which continues as Rakoci ut. Both sides of these streets are lined with shops and department stores with a broad range of goods.

More fun for most visitors is the pedestrian precinct with up-market fashion shops and coffee bars centring on Vaci Street from Vorosmarty Square to Kigyo Street and Petofi Sandor Street. This area is Budapest's Bond Street. It's also a pleasant place for an evening stroll, when the shops are closed but you can still window-gaze at the lively displays. Special for capitalists who want to buy bonds: the former Eastern bloc's first Stock Exchange opened on Vaci Street in 1990.

Across the river in the Castle District, high-quality boutiques and folk-art shops are geared to tourism, and charge ambitious prices. There is wide range of fashion accessories. Look, for instance, at the choice of hand-crafted ear-rings.

Opening hours

Most stores are open from 9 or 10 a.m., markets from 6 a.m. Closing times are mostly at 18 hrs. (20 hrs for food departments); and 20 hrs on Thursdays, 13 hrs on Saturdays. Basic supermarkets are open from 7-20 hrs; Saturday 7-14 hrs. All are closed on Sundays except for morning markets in some suburban areas.

Department Stores and Shopping Centres
Luxus Department Store, Vaci Street
Aranypok Department Store, Vaci Street
Florian Shopping Centre, 111 Florian ter 6-9
Skala Co-op Department Store, XI Schonherz Zu. 6-10
Sugar Shopping Centre, XIV Ors vezer ter
Skala-Metro, Marx Ter – opposite Western Railway
Station

You can also purchase a select range of Hungarian goods in
International tourist shops. These are mainly located in
hotels and accept only hard currency or credit cards.
Folk Art: Konsumtourist shops in hotels; or at Folk Art
Shop (Nepmuveszeti bolt) V, Vaci ut 14; or XIII Szt Istvan
krt 26.

Markets
In search of local colour (and local produce), most people
enjoy visiting a bustling market to glimpse everyday life
among average Hungarians. Several excellent markets are
scattered through Budapest. Easily the most interesting
and accessible is the Central Marketing Hall in District IX,
at Tolbuhin korut 103. Hundreds of stalls are ranged
along six covered avenues, 500 feet long.

By Western standards, the prices for all the farm and
market-garden products seem very low. With flash you
can get amusing photos of sausage and salami displays,
dairy products, garlic and hanging strings of dazzling-red
paprika.

One can reach this central marketing place by taking a
No. 2 tram along the river embankment, and get off at
Szabadsag Bridge. The Central Marketing Hall is then just
across the square. Highly recommended!

4.9 Eating Out
The Hungarian people enjoy life and this is especially
evident when it comes to eating and drinking. Even
smaller restaurants offer menus with up to 50 or 60 items
every day. The food is excellent, and served in generous
portions at low prices by West European standards.
Service is quick and friendly.

All eating places must offer at least two set menus each
day, by law. These inexpensive tourist menus generally
include soup, a main course and dessert. However, you
will rarely find a translation, and waiters prefer to lure you
into the à la carte side of the menu.

Service charge is not usually included in the price unless
indicated on the menu and a minimum 15% tip is
customary. Many restaurants feature live music during
the evening meal – especially gipsy violinists who play
from table to table, and expect a 100-Forint banknote at
each stop.

83

Here's a rough guide to prices:
Something like 300 Forints to 500 for an average set menu. Soups cost from 30 to 150 Ft depending on the restaurant, and the ingredients. Fish soup is at the more expensive end.

Starters go from 100 to 800 or 900 Ft. The most expensive starters are goose liver, or Russian caviare. Salads go from 50 to 100 Ft. Main courses are especially variations on pork, with a price-range from 200 to 800 Ft.

Wines: the most expensive is Tokaj, costing 600 to 800 Ft for a half-litre bottle. Other wines in standard size bottles go from 350 to 500 Ft in a restaurant.

Hungary has more visitors speaking German than any other language, so that's the usual second language. Many menus have only a German translation. But more up-market eating places also have English menus, and waiters who can cope with English.

For a simple lunch, there are hundreds of low-cost fast-food and self-service establishments around town, where you can look and point. Bakeries make up very tempting sandwiches and portions of pizza.

For a more memorable meal, here's a short list of restaurants that serve traditional food. Reservations are recommended at weekends.

District 1 – Castle District
Most of the restaurants in this area cater specially for the tourist trade, with plenty of atmosphere, multi-lingual waiters and gipsy musicians.

Fortuna, 1, Hess Andras ter 4   Tel: 1756 857
One of the oldest and most elegant in the castle district, by the Hilton Hotel. The first book printed in Hungary was published here in 1473, and the building later housed the University Press. Open: 12-16 & 19-01 hrs.

Alabardos Restaurant, 1, Orszaghaz utca 2
Tel: 1560 851
In a 16th Century building by the Hilton Hotel, an elegant first-class candle-lit restaurant with medieval furnishings. Open: 19-24 hrs.

Regi Orszaghaz, Orszaghaz utca 17   Tel: 1750 650
"The Old Parliament Building", near Hilton Hotel. On the ground floor it's a regular restaurant serving Hungarian dishes with gipsy music. Downstairs is a wine-cellar offering extremely simple food, like bread and fat, and you drink wine.

Aranyszarvas, 1, Szarvas ter 1   Tel: 1756 451
"The Golden Deer" specialises in venison and other game, on Buda side near Elizabeth Bridge.

District V – Inner City
All the principal hotels have excellent dining rooms, with

first-class service. In the surrounding streets, numerous good restaurants cater for visitors and locals alike.

Restaurant Pilvax, V, Pilvaz Koz 1-3

Tel: 1176 396

The original restaurant was a coffee house that was a meeting place for revolutionary groups. The Hungarian revolution of 1848 started from here. Open: 12-24 hrs; Sun 12-16 hrs.

Legradi testverek, V, Magyar utca 23

Tel: 1186 804

"The Legradi Brothers" is in a small street near the Astoria Hotel. Very luxurious and expensive, for trendy diplomats and rich tourists, with golden spoon service. Open: 17-24 hrs. Closed Sat & Sun.

Szazeves, V, Pesti Barnabas utca 2   Tel: 1183 608

"Century" restaurant, claimed as the oldest in Budapest, operating in a small building that is a listed monument, near Vaci Street and Elizabeth Bridge. Good food, gipsy music, traditional atmosphere. Open: 12-24 hrs.

Menes Csarda, V, Apaczai Csere Janos utca 15

Tel: 1170 803

First class Hungarian music and cuisine. Located by the Atrium Hyatt. Open: 12-16 hrs & 18-24 hrs.

Matyas Pince, V, Marcius 15 ter 7   Tel: 1181 650

Established 1904, just by Elizabeth Bridge. Among the traditional specialities are Bridegroom's Soup, and varied carp dishes. Music is played every evening by gipsies of the Sandor Latakos clan. Open: 11-01 hrs.

Off-centre restaurants

Hungaria, VII, Lenin korut 9-11   Tel: 1223 849

A restaurant and coffee house, it's a traditional meeting place for poets and writers, and is famous for Hungarian and international cuisine. Open: 9-22 hrs.

Disznofo, XII, Szilassy utca 18   Tel: 1559 765

"Head of a Wild Boar" between the Buda Hills – hunting-lodge atmosphere with traditional meals.

Etoile, XIII, Pozsonyi ut 4   Tel: 1122 242

Near Margit Bridge, French and national cuisine. First class atmosphere, turn of the century. Open 12-15 hrs & 18-01 hrs.

Gundel Restaurant, XIV, Allatkerti korut 2

Tel: 1221 002

In the Heroes Square district, one of the most famous in Budapest serving international and Hungarian cuisine. Gundel pancakes were invented here. Expensive. Mrs

Thatcher dined at Gundel's in 1984. Open: 12-16 &
19-24 hrs.

Beer-Halls

A number of Gold Fassl, Tuborg, Gösser and other
brand-name beer-halls are spread through Budapest. They
serve bottled and draught beer and a range of pub snacks.
Here are two that are worth sampling:

Kaltenberg Bavarian Royal Beerhall, IX., Kinizsi utca
30.
Emke, VII., Lenin korut 2.

Coffee Bars and Pastry Shops

Hungarians have the coffee and cake habit, just as deeply
as the Viennese. Cafés and pastry shops flourish in the city
centre. Among the pastry specialities, try Retes – thin
pastry or Strudel with choice of fillings: almas (apple);
meggyes (sour cherry); makos (poppy seed); turos (cottage
cheese). Pancakes (palacsinta) likewise come with a wide
range of fillings. The gourmet speciality is Gundel
Palacsinta – filled with a nut and raisin paste, drenched in a
creamy chocolate rum sauce and then flambéed.

For the full rich experience of a Hungarian pastry shop,
go to **Gerbeaud**, V, Vorosmarty ter 7. Founded in 1858,
Gerbeaud is the most famous café and patisserie in
Hungary. Very central, it also serves ice-cream and
sandwiches. Usually very busy, with fitful service. Open
9-21 hrs.

Hungarian specialities

Komenymag	Caraway seed
leves	soup with
nokedival	dumplings
Hideg almaleves	Cold apple soup
Libamaj pastetom	A goose liver paté with brandy
Hortobagyi husos	Thin pancakes filled with minced
palacsinta	pork stew and dressed with sour cream
Paprika szeketej	Sliced green peppers, ewe's
korozottel toltve	cheese, spices and a dash of beer
Gulyasleves	Chunks of beef, potatoes, onion,
(goulash soup)	tomatoes and peppers with paprika, caraway seeds and garlic (what is called goulash abroad is actually a meat stew called porkolt.
Szegedi halaszle	Freshwater bouillabaisse with paprika
Balatoni fogas	Pike-perch (considered a prime delicacy)
Csikos tokany	Strips of beef braised in diced

	bacon, onions, sliced pepper and tomatoes served with miniature dumplings
Toltott Kaposzta	Soured cabbage leaves stuffed with minced meat and rice cooked with sauerkraut and served with sour cream
Toltott paprika	Stuffed pepper
Paprikas csirke	Paprika chicken
Fatanyeros	Mixed grill; several kinds of meat with garnish and salad served on a platter
Rablohus	Served on a brochette; pork, bacon, potatoes and onion
Paprikas krumpli	Paprika potatoes often served with sausages or frankfurters

Guide to menu items

If the menu has a German translation, you'll probably do better with the menu guide in Chapter One.

Soups & starters:

Bableves	Bean soup
Bakonyi betyarleves	Outlaw soup
Bekacomb	Frog's legs
Eroleves	Consomme
Gyumolcsle	Fruit juice
Husgomboccal	With meat & dumplings
Leves	Soup
Husleves	Meat soup

Main courses & snacks:

Baranyhus	Lamb
Borda	Chop
Borjuhus	Veal
Csirke	Chicken
Csuka	Pike
Diszohus	Pork
Fasirozott	Meatballs
Felfujt	Soufflé
Fogas	Pike-Perch
Galuska	Dumplings
Gulyasleves	Goulash (soup)
Hal	Fish
Halsalata	Fish salad
Hus	Meat
Kacsa	Duck
Kappan	Capon
Kolbaszfelek	Sausages
Liba	Goose
Marhahus	Beef
Metelt	Noodles

Nyul	Rabbit
Ponty	Carp
Porkolt	Stew
Pulyka	Turkey
Raksalata	Crab salad
Rizs	Rice
Rostelyos	Stewed steak
Sonka	Ham
Szendvics	Sandwich

Vegetables:

Burgonya	Potatoes
Fokhagyma	Garlic
Fozelek	Vegetables
Gomba	Mushrooms
Hagyma	Onions
Kaposzta	Cabbage
Paradicsom	Tomatoes
Salata	Lettuce or salad
Sargarepa	Carrots
Sultkrumpli	Chips
Uborka	Cucumber
Vegyesfozelek	Mixed vegetables
Zeller	Celery
Zoldborso	Peas

Desserts:

Alma	Apple
Aranygaluska	Sweet dumpling
Ananasz	Pineapple
Citrom	Lemon
Cseresznye	Cherries
Eper	Strawberries
Fagylalt	Ice-cream
Gorogdinnye	Watermelon
Malna	Raspberries
Meggy	Sour cherries
Narancs	Orange
Oszibarack	Peach
Palacsinta	Pancakes
Ribizli	Red currants
Sargabarack	Apricot
Sajt	Cheese

Miscellaneous:

Cukor	Sugar
Dio	Nuts
Edeskomeny	Caraway seeds
Kenyer	Bread
Mustar	Mustard
So	Salt
Vaj	Butter

Drinks:

Asvany-viz	Mineral water
Bor	Wine
Froccs	Half-wine, half-soda
Gyumolcsle	Fruit juice
Italok	Drinks
Kapuciner	Capuccino
Kave	Coffee
Limonade	Lemonade
Soda-viz	Soda water
Sor	Beer
Tea	Tea
Tej	Milk
Viz	Water

Some cooking terms:

Dinsztelve	Braised
Fove	Broiled
Rantva	Breaded
Sulve	Roasted
Sutve	Fried
Toltott	Stuffed

4.10 Nightlife

Budapest offers nightlife to suit all tastes ranging from opera, ballet, symphony concerts and chamber music to rock and jazz, nightclubs, discos and bars. New theatrical productions are premiered every week.

Most nights Hungarian dancers perform in national costume at the MOM Cultural Centre (XII, Csorsz utsa 18) or at the Municipal Cultural Centre (XI, Fehervari ut 47). Tickets are available on the spot, or at the Central Booking Office (VI, Andrassy ut 18).

Hungary has a rich culture, and national pride ensures that Liszt, Kodaly and Bartok get a frequent hearing – especially those works that are based on folk melodies. Many Austrians come regularly to Budapest for musical events, which are so much less expensive than in Vienna.

Standards are high at the two opera houses and three concert halls. There are opera or ballet performances every night during the winter season. Reserved seats can easily be booked from Vienna. Otherwise get tickets through your hotel or travel-agency rep; or from the Central Booking Office above.

Every year a 10-day Spring Festival is scheduled in late March, with about a thousand different events around the city.

When opera houses and concert halls close for the summer, the Margaret Island open-air theatre, amongst others, takes over. The season re-opens late September onwards with autumn Music Weeks.

Goulash Party

A popular tourist entertainment is dinner at a traditional restaurant with goulash, strudel, Hungarian wines, folklore displays and gipsy music. The musicians do their soulful best, with languishing gipsy melody, to reduce the entire clientele to wistful melancholia. Then, when the tears are almost ready to flow, they set you afire with a whirling, exciting folk-dance. Not to be missed!

River cruises

Another variation on the goulash party theme is to take an evening Danube Cruise with dinner, wine, music and folklore show. At first the cost may seem rather high. But you travel on a very comfortable boat and the gipsy band is first-class – normally a lead violin, a cello, a cymbalom, a clarinet and a bass. As Budapest lights up, you get splendid views of a capital that sparkles. Other evening cruises are available, with or without music or food.

Nightclubs, cabarets and discos

Balloon – Hotel Atrium Hyatt, V Roosevelt ter 2

Casanova Bar – 1 Batthyany ter 4

Gipsy Cocktail Bar – Hotel Duna Intercontinental, V Apaczai Csere Ju 4

Maxime Varieté – Hotel Emke, VII, Akacfa utca 3

Moulin Rouge – VI, Nagymezo utca 17

4.11 At your service

Money & Banking

The Hungarian currency is the forint (Ft). One forint divides into 100 fillers, like splitting the atom. Coins are of 1, 2, 5, 10 and 20 Ft. Notes are 10, 20, 50, 100, 500 and 1,000 Ft. You are allowed to bring maximum of 100 Forints into the country.

Changing money

The exchange rate is the same everywhere: at the Hungarian National Bank, National Savings Bank (OTP) branches, exchange desks at travel and tourist offices and at hotels. Banking hours are normally Monday to Friday 9-17 hrs; Saturdays 9-14 hrs. In high season, you can also change money at the Posta Bank on Saturdays and Sundays, from 9-13 hrs.

Produce your passport when changing money. Street deals with private citizens are not legal, and light-fingered black marketeers could easily leave you holding a bundle of toilet paper.

Keep your exchange dockets. On leaving Hungary you may re-exchange only a maximum of half the amount indicated on receipts.

Post Office and Telephone

Opening hours – generally from 8-18 hours Monday to Friday and 8-12 hrs on Saturdays. Main offices operate from 7-20 hrs. Stamps can be bought quicker from tobacconists, Monday to Friday. Post boxes are painted red and mail is collected every few hours.

Other services offered by the post office are telephone, telegraph and telex services, but not money transfers. If you want to make a long-distance or international phone call, find a kiosk where the equipment inside is painted red. Call boxes with yellow fittings are for local calls only.

International phone calls: insert at least 10 Ft coin in the slot. For dialling codes, see section 1.3 of this book. An international telecommunications centre operates from 7-20 hrs Monday to Friday and until 19 hrs on Saturdays at the corner of Petofi andor utca and Martinelli ter (Budapest V). Linguists are also on duty here. For directory enquiries in English tel: 1172-200.

Calls within Budapest: insert a 2 Ft coin in the slot and dial the number. Daytime the yellow city phones give you three minutes for 2 Forints. From 18 hrs till 7 a.m. you get six minutes for 2 Ft.

All Budapest phone numbers from September 1989 have an extra '1' added at the start, to make a seven-digit number. If you are using an older reference book with 6-figure numbers, just stick a '1' in front.

Emergency telephone numbers

Police	07
Fire Brigade	05
Ambulance	04

Other phone numbers, and addresses

Police Headquarters, also dealing with passports
1061 Budapest VI, Nepkoztarsasag utja 12
Check opening times first!

Lost Property
Central lost property office
Bp. V Engels ter 5. Tel: 1174-961 Open: Mon 8-18 hrs; Tues to Thurs 8-17; Fri 8-15; Sat Closed.

Losses on Public Transport:
BKV office, Bp. VII Akacfa u 18   Tel: 1226-613
Open: Mon Tues & Thurs 7-16 hrs; Wed & Fri 07.00-18.30; Sat Closed
Note: Passports and other personal documents handed into the Lost Property Office are transferred to KEOKH (Aliens Registration Office) at Police HQ – address above.

Medical

Budapest is one of Europe's leading spa cities. Many people come to regain their health at one of the therapeutic baths. However, in case of an accident or sudden illness the Hungarian National Health Service (S.Z.T.K.) and the emergency squad (Mentok) are very capable at handling any unexpected problems.

Most Hungarian doctors and dentists also have private practices, at which payment is required for consultations. Keep receipts for any travel insurance claim. To find an English-speaking doctor or dentist, ask at hotel reception. Your consulate can also name suitable local doctors.

Pharmaceutical chemists

Look for the sign *gyogyszertar* or *patika*. These shops only sell pharmaceutical and related products. For toiletries go to an *illatszerbolt* and for films to a *fotoszakuzlet*. Some chemists remain open all night. Their addresses can be found on an illuminated sign displayed in other chemists' windows.

24-hour service:

91 Lenin Korut 1067	22 Frankel Leo ut 1027
86 Rakoczi ut 1074	3 Boraros ter 1093

Embassies

Great Britain, V Harmincad u 6	Tel: 1182-888
USA, Szabadsag ter 12	Tel: 1124-224
Canada, 11 Budakeszi ut 53/d	Tel: 1165-858

Tourist Information

For information by telephone in English call TOURIN-FORM on 1179-800. The service operates from 7-21 hrs Monday to Friday; to 20 hrs on Saturdays and 8-13 hrs on Sundays. The office is located at Sütö u. 2, next to Deak Square.

Hungary's leading travel agency is Ibusz, with numerous offices in and near hotels, railway stations, busy shopping areas and at the airport. They operate during normal office hours. However, during summer many of the offices are open until 20 or 22 hrs.

News

The Hungarians broadcast an English language service called Radio Bridge on FM 102.1. It's a round-the-clock programme which carries the Voice of America news reports and features. Buy the Daily News, a four-page English-language newspaper produced by the Hungarian News Agency, which uses its own news agency reports and also Reuters, AP and other international news agencies. This newspaper carries the daily Radio Bridge timings.

Most of the leading hotels offer television, with international programmes by satellite.

Chapter Five

Prague

5.1 City of dreaming spires

Prague ranks high among the more beautiful capitals of
Europe, and happily was relatively untouched by two
World Wars. Sited on the River Vltava – itself a lyrical
theme for painters and musicians – it's a city of a hundred
spires that dominate the skyline.

There's enough to keep a sightseer busy for several
days. Prague abounds in picturesque old streets that wind
up steep cobbled hillsides, with Hradcany Castle as the
highlight. Palaces are preserved as museums. There is
plentiful mixture of Baroque, Gothic and Renaissance
architecture.

For many years, owing to other priorities, Prague had a
dilapidated, run-down appearance. But in more recent
times public buildings have been given a major face-lift.
The blackened grime of past decades has been scrubbed
away, to reveal the beautiful pastel colours of the original
stonework. The clean-up continues.

By night, Prague offers good opportunities for opera
and ballet, orchestral and chamber music, puppet shows.
Leading hotels feature Western-style night-clubs and
dancing, with reasonable prices unless you order drinks
imported from hard-currency countries.

For a quieter drink, there are some elegant bars with
suave service. At the other extreme are noisy smoke-filled
beer taverns and cellars where devotees weigh up the
merits of the great variety of different brews.

Prague is a good base for excursions through a countryside of tranquil rivers, pine-clad hills, historic castles and
picture-book farmhouses and villages, well-painted and
trim. Smetana's tone-poem "Ma Vlast" (My Country)
gives a musical picture of Bohemia's serenity, little
changed by the 20th century.

Many castles are located in the area. Among the finest is
Hluboka. Sited 250 feet above the Vltava, it is modelled
on England's Windsor Castle, and contains a superb
collection of tapestry, furniture and arms.

In general, out-of-pocket expenses on meals, transport
and entertainment are extremely low when calculated at
current exchange rates. Room tariffs at hotels are closer to
Western levels.

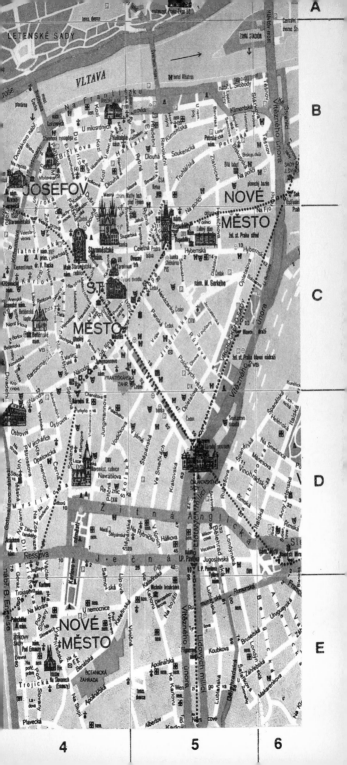

Since the dramatic political events of December 1989, moves towards a market economy are changing many of the former subsidised prices. Exchange rates are likewise under review. But visitors during the 90's will probably continue to enjoy low-level expenses, with all the fascination of seeing Prague under new management.

5.2 Arrival & hotel

By air, London Heathrow to Prague is served daily by either British Airways or Czechoslovak Airlines. For two-centre travellers, there are daily flights from Vienna by Czechoslovak Airlines or Austrian Airlines. By train from Vienna's Franz Josef Bahnhof takes $5\frac{1}{2}$ hours, or about the same by motor-coach.

Visas for British passport-holders have been abolished since October 1990. Currently the rules of entry and currency control are under review, so check the latest details from your travel agency; or from the Czechoslovak Embassy at 28 Kensington Palace Gardens, London W8 4QY – Tel: 071-727 3966; or from Cedok in London, at 17/18 Old Bond Street, W1X 4RB. Tel: 071-629 6058.

Cedok is the largest Czechoslovak travel organisation. Their offices and reps are available for any advice or information you may require whilst in Prague. They provide a currency exchange service, and can book any of the excursions available.

Cedok representatives are available at the following places:

Airport: Cedok desk. Normally open Mon-Fri 7-18 hrs. Sat-Sun 8-16 hrs.

Cedok Head Office: British Departments – Na prikope 18, Prague 1. Tel: 212 7637.

If you are making your own way by taxi to or from the airport, expect to pay about £5 for a journey time of about 30 minutes.

Hotel grades can compare with those of West-European countries, but rooms are in short supply. In the centre, elderly hotels like the Ambassador, Esplanade and Palace have mostly been modernised, while keeping their traditional atmosphere. Indeed, the Palace Hotel has been totally rebuilt inside the original facade, and has moved up to luxury grade.

With a basic policy of preserving the historic appearance of the city centre, the modern international style of high-rise glass and concrete has been kept a decent distance away. The Intercontinental on the river bank does not obtrude. But the high-rise Forum Praha is several Metro stops away from the centre. Three botels are moored by the river bank to help ease the bed shortage.

5.3 Getting around Prague
Public transport
Most of the city hotels are within easy stroll of the tourist areas. Visitors need make very little use of public transport, which operates between 5.30 and midnight every day! Elderly trams trundle and clank to all corners of Prague, with numerous bus services as a back-up. The centre is also well served by a modern Metro system. Ticket prices have recently increased, but are still incredibly low – the same price regardless of distance. On a three-day visit, it's hard to spend even a pound total on inner-city transport.

Buses and trams are very easy to use. Your hotel staff or tour rep will give advice on direct routes. Tickets must be bought in advance from hotel receptions, tobacconists, newsagents and Metro stations. There are no conductors, so you must punch your own ticket. Don't forget, as there are occasional controls. Anyone without a validated ticket gets an on-the-spot fine. Use a fresh ticket each time you change.

Metro
The standard fare covers the entire journey, regardless of any changes. There are three lines:

A – which runs East to West

B and C – which both run North to South.

At the subway entrance, insert your coin at the turnstile and walk through. If you don't have the right coin, there are normally machines inside the station which make change. To plan your route, look for the last station on the line. This gives you the name of the line to follow.

Look for the words VSTUP = Entrance; VYSTUP = Exit.

Taxis
Cheap but elusive! Radio cabs take ages to arrive. During the day, taxis are more prevalent and often lurk near the big hotels. If you need a taxi late at night, check how much the journey will cost, and even haggle! Taxis have meters which don't always work for foreign visitors.

Car Hire
Cedok at Na prikope 18 can arrange a rented car. You need an International Driver's Permit.

5.4 Basic Prague
Most of sightseeing Prague is comfortably within walking distance. On a short visit, the following check-list covers the highlights.

(1)   Explore Hradcany Castle and the Golden Lane of the medieval alchemists.

(2)   Take a trip by paddle steamer on the Vltava.

(3)   On the hour, see and hear the performance of the medieval clock on the Old Town Hall.

(4)   Saunter along Charles Bridge among the craft workers and entertainers.

(5)   Enjoy an out-of-town coach excursion to see historic castles and the beautiful Czech countryside.

(6)   Wander at random into ancient courtyards and alleys in the central area around the Old Town Hall Square.

(7)   For a most unusual theatre experience, try to get tickets for the 'Laterna Magika' show.

(8)   Pay homage at the informal memorial to Jan Palach in Wenceslas Square.

(9)   Inspect Bohemia crystal and Carlsbad porcelain at Moser on Na prikope.

(10) Sample different brews at the U Fleku beer-house.

Orientation

Sightseers' Prague comprises four main centres of attraction on the city map – two on each side of the River Vltava which flows through the capital. Eight river islands are mostly used for sporting activities.

Dominating the skyline is the hilltop Hradcany district: the Castle, several aristocratic palaces, the tall silhouette of St Vitus Cathedral and a delightful Golden Lane that reputedly was an R&D centre for medieval alchemists.

At the foot of the Hradcany complex is Mala Strana, the Lesser Town: a Prague Baroque district of 17th- and 18th-century mansions and embassies, with the Jesuit Saint Nicholas Church overlooking the central square called Malostranske namesti. Traditional coffeehouses and restaurants are numerous in this area, which is also a principal stopping-point for buses and trams.

Out of the fifteen bridges which cross the Vltava, the tourist favourite is the 14th-century Charles Bridge, one of the oldest and most decorative stone bridges of central Europe.

Directly opposite is Karlova Street, lined with splendid town houses and winding towards the Town Hall Square (Starometske namesti), which is the fabulous centrepiece of Stare Mesto or Old Town. Down the wide Paris Street (Parizka) leads back to the river at the Intercontinental Hotel – starting point for Cedok sightseeing tours. Close by is the former ghetto which includes the oldest existing synagogue in Europe: one of the buildings which forms part of the Jewish National Museum. Another direction from the Town Hall Square leads along Celetna Street to the Powder Tower. This was the Royal Road taken by Bohemian kings when they went in state procession to Prague Castle to be crowned.

Powder Tower stands at one end of Na prikope, the lively shopping street which follows the line of the former moat between Old and New Towns. At the other end of Na prikope is a statue of Masaryk – first President of the Czechoslovak Republic – at the bottom of Wenceslas Square. Here was the scene of the demonstrations of December 1989 which led to collapse of Communist government. The New Town is the principal area of shops, restaurants and hotels.

All four areas are pedestrianized, so that sightseeing on foot is a jay-walker's paradise. You can easily link up Prague's highlights with almost nil possibility of being stabbed in the back by a Skoda motor-car.

Prague Castle, Hradcany

By public transport, take a tram or Metro to Malostranska, then tram 22 uphill to Hradcany and follow the crowds to Hradcanske namesti. This square was centre of the original Hradcany town, and has retained its basic medieval layout. Around this elegant approach to Prague Castle are mansions and palaces, mostly 16th century Renaissance style. On the right, at No. 2 next to St Benedict's Church, is the mid-16th century **Schwarzenberg Palace** which today houses the Museum of Military History. No. 5 is Tuscany Palace with an Early Baroque facade. No. 1 is Salm Palace, now the Swiss Embassy.

Walk towards the Castle gates. To the right is a superb viewpoint over the city, while back to the left is the long facade of Cernin Palace, founded in 17th century but largely rebuilt about 60 years ago. It now houses the Ministry of Foreign Affairs.

Enter the ceremonial gates into Prague Castle, founded in the 9th century. A Romanesque palace was built on the site in the 12th century, and has been rebuilt or reconstructed several times since. In 14th century the Castle became a royal residence, but later served mainly as a centre of government. With establishment of the Czechoslovak Republic in 1918, Hradcany became the President's official seat. However, President Havel has chosen not to live in the Castle, but in his private home. Reception rooms are used for State occasions and are not open to the public.

Cathedral of St Vitus

In the third courtyard of Prague Castle stands the cathedral, founded in year 926. The present Gothic building dates from 14th century, and was designed by a French architect. The steeple was completed in 1562, while the Baroque roof dates from 1770. Final completion of the cathedral was in 1929.

Something like the Westminster Abbey of Prague, St Vitus Cathedral has been the setting for all big State occasions, the burial place of princes and kings, and the treasury for the Bohemian crown jewels.

Good King Wenceslas – St Vaclav – is buried in the Wenceslas Chapel, which was constructed between 1347 and 1366. He was the good king who helped spread Christianity during his reign from 920–929. He was then assassinated by his brother, who disliked the mixing of religion with practical politics. The martyred King Wenceslas later became the patron saint of Bohemia, and is the favourite symbol today of Czech unity against foreign influence. His chapel is decorated with frescoes and semi-precious stones.

Vikarska Street

Along the north side of the Cathedral is the narrow but charming Vikarska Street, which has changed little from past centuries. The Vikarka restaurant and wine tavern is housed in the former Old and New Vicarages, which adjoin the Old Deanery. The restaurant is partly built into the Castle fortifications.

St George's Basilica

Behind the Cathedral is George Square with a splendid basilica founded in 920 and completed in the 12th century. St George's Basilica is the best-preserved Romanesque building in Bohemia.

Golden Lane

Further down, reached by a little turning to the left, is the favourite tourist haunt of Golden Lane. It's a group of tiny medieval houses which formerly were the haunt of alchemists, trying to turn base metal into gold. They have now been converted into enticing little shops that transmute souvenirs and antiques into hard currency.
Open: Nov-Mar 9-16 hrs; Apr-Oct 9-17 hrs.

The Lesser Town – Mala Strana

Walking down from Prague Castle brings you into the Mala Strana district of town mansions, picturesque side streets and Prague Baroque monuments. Centre of the district is Malostranske namesti. Many of the buildings have dingy and crumbling facades, but work continues to restore them to their original colourful condition.

New Town Hall, Malostranske namesti

Of the original Gothic structure, only the cellars and double colonnade of the ground floor have been preserved.

St Nicholas Church, Malostranske namesti

The most outstanding example of Bohemian Baroque in Prague, completed in 1755. Open: 9-16 hrs.

Wallenstein Palace and Garden, Valdstejnske namesti
One of the finest Baroque-style palaces in Prague, built
1623–1630. From May to September the gardens are
open daily except Monday, through an entrance in
Letenska Street, 10-18 hrs.

Charles Bridge

Charles Bridge must rate very high among the top ten
tourist-interest bridges of Europe. A pedestrian bridge,
highly popular with visitors and residents alike, it offers
delight in all seasons. Viewpoints and photo possibilities
open up almost everywhere you look. Dating from 1357,
the bridge parapets are lined with thirty Baroque statues
and groups which were added in early 18th century.
Buskers and craft peddlers crowd the bridge, end to end.
On fine summer days, it can easily take half an hour to
work past all the distractions. The bridge is named after
Charles IV, greatest of the Czech kings.

The Old Town – Stary Mesto

Focal point of the historic trading centre of Prague is the
Old Town Square – Staromestske namesti – which
originated in 10th century as a broad marketplace. In the
middle of the cobbled expanse is a very large monument
to John Huss – Jan Hus – the Czech religious reformer who
was greatly influenced by England's John Wycliffe.

Dominating the square are the twin towers of **Tyn
Church** – an Early Gothic triple-naved building that
dates mainly from mid-14th century. For years it was
wrapped in scaffolding while renovations continued; but
entry is now possible.

Just before every hour through the day, crowds con-
gregate outside the Old Town Hall, to see a performance
of the **Astronomical Clock**. Built by a master watchmaker
in 1410, it's the oldest of its kind in Europe to be still
operating. Two upper windows open on the stroke of
every hour, to unleash a procession of the 12 apostles.
Below the windows is an astronomical sphere which
indicates the three different times used in the Middle
Ages. Standing on each side are figures representing
human vanity and miserliness, a skeleton and the figure of
a Turk.

From the Town Hall's arched entrance alongside,
wedding parties surge out at intervals from their civil
ceremonies. Horse-carriage rides start from the other side.
Year-round there's always something happening in the
Old Town Square, making it a great meeting-place. In
mid-summer craft workers give on-the-spot demonstrations; or possibly a historical fencing group will give a
theatrical display against a backdrop of the pastel-coloured
buildings. In December the square is setting for a traditional
Christmas market.

The square and its surrounding streets and courtyards are well supplied with cafés, restaurants and ale-houses, making it a delightful area for an evening stroll by gaslight in search of food and refreshment.

Each of the radiating streets leads to other points of interest in the Old Town. The little square of Male namesti funnels into Karlova, which goes direct to Charles Bridge. Melantrichova or Zelezna streets take you through to Wenceslas Square and Na prikope. Celetna is the superbly reconstructed Royal Road leading to the Powder Tower. Parizska – a street of airline offices – goes to the former Jewish ghetto and to the Intercontinental Hotel.

Na prikope

Na prikope came into existence only in the 18th century, when the Old Town moat was filled in. Covering the short distance between the Powder Tower and Wenceslas Square, Na prikope has been greatly improved by the removal of tram lines and opening of a pedestrian precinct.

Good shops, restaurants and cafés have made this into the liveliest of Prague streets. For lunch break, try the first-class Russian restaurant Moskva at No. 29 on the first floor, or the Russian self-service below, called Arbat. Prices are very modest. Several pavement cafés operate during summer months.

In this area you can also experience the old-time coffeehouse scene. By the Powder Tower, Na prikope opens into a square called Namesti Republiky. The next building is Obecni dum – Municipal House – which features a very large traditional Kavarna, with outdoor seating in fine weather. Inside is more interesting, where you can sample a fattening range of ices and cream cakes in a 19th-century setting. As part of the complex of concert halls and meeting rooms, there's also a very large restaurant, with reasonable prices; and a basement wine cellar.

Wenceslas Square

Over half a mile long and seventy yards wide, Wenceslas Square has flourished as the town's principal thoroughfare, shopping and social centre, ever since Charles IV founded the New Town in 1348. At first it was called Horse Market, but the name was changed to Wenceslas Square in 1848 – though the Good King's present statue was not erected until 1912.

Like Na prikope, Wenceslas Square has been greatly improved in recent years by banishing tramcars and converting most of the boulevard into a pedestrian precinct. With so many windows for shop-gazing, sedate hotels and intriguing arcades and courtyards, it's certainly worth exploring both sides of the avenue during your Prague City Break. Well-tended flower displays line the central promenade. At the top end the National Museum dominates the background to St. Wenceslas.

Just below the statue has become a place of political pilgrimage. An informal shrine is dedicated to Jan Palach, the student who burned himself to death in protest at Soviet occupation. His photograph – and those of other leaders from Czechoslovakia's recent history – is always surrounded by fresh flowers and burning candles.

5.5. Other sights

Buildings and Monuments

Bethlehem Chapel, Betlemske namesti, Prague 1.
Gothic Chapel completed in 1391. The Czech religious reformer John Huss preached here in the years 1402-13.
Open: 9-18 hrs (April-September); 9-17 hrs (October).
Closed: November-March.

Powder Tower – Prasna brana, Celetna Street
Gothic tower built 1475. It's the only tower remaining from the original fortifications of Prague Old Town. Views over central Prague are well worth the effort of climbing three lots of narrow spiral stairs. Open: only during summer season, on Sat, Sun and public holidays. Apr and Oct 10-17 hrs; May-Sep 10-18 hrs.

Royal Summer Palace – Kralovsky lethohradek,
Belvedere
Renaissance palace built in 1535–1563. The gardens contain a bronze 'singing fountain' cast in 1568. Open: Daily except Monday, 10-18 hrs.

Emmaus – Emauzy, Na Slovanech, Prague 2
Former monastery of the Slavonic Benedictines, founded mid-14th century. Badly damaged in 1945, it has since been reconstructed.

The Clementinium, Krizonvrucke nam. 4
A Baroque building dating from mid-17th century. Originally a Jesuit college, it now houses the Czech State Library.

Museums and Galleries

National Museum, Vaclavske namesti 68
Dominating the top end of Wenceslas Square: the oldest museum in Prague, housing geological, zoological, prehistoric, historic and cultural collections.
Open: 9-16 hrs. Closed: Tuesday.

Antonin Dvorak Museum, Ke Karlovu 20, Prague 2
Dedicated to the composer's life.
Open: 10-17 hrs. Closed: Monday.

103

National Technology Museum, Kostelni 42, Prague 7
Exhibition of Czech technology.
Open: 9-17 hrs. Closed: Monday

Prague Ghetto (Old Jewish quarter) – located in streets
around Cervena and Parizka, near Inter-Continental Hotel.
A few monuments have survived from the old Prague
ghetto, including the 13th century early Gothic Synagogue.

State Jewish Museum, 3 Jachymova
Objects displayed here were collected by the Nazis.
Open: 9-17 hrs. Closed Saturday.

5.6 Take a trip

There is great beauty in the Czech countryside around the
capital – rolling hills, woodlands, fields, small villages and
scattered farmhouses. Within one-day touring range are
several historic castles which add great sightseeing interest
to the scenic pleasures, especially southwards. By rented
car you can explore the region, or choose from a selection
of coach tours.

Prime destinations are:

Karlstejn – 20 miles out from Prague, along the Vltava
and Berounka valleys. In a magnificent forest setting, the
Bohemian Gothic castle was founded in 1348 by Charles
IV to guard the royal treasures and crown jewels. It rates
as one of Czechoslovakia's most important monuments.

Slapy Lake – a blissful recreational area created by Slapy
dam on the River Vltava. There are direct buses from
Prague.

Konopiste – Long avenues of trees lead to this castle
which was almost totally rebuilt from 1887 by Archduke
Franz Ferdinand, heir to the Austrian throne and later
assassinated at Sarajevo. He was dedicated to hunting, and
kept a detailed account-book of his lifetime's 300,000
bag, with sub-totals for every species of animal or bird.
Large numbers of the trophies fill the walls. The castle also
houses a great collection of arms from 15th and 16th
centuries.

Orlik – A dam on the Vltava has created a 40-mile lake,
very popular for canoeists and fishermen. Two castles can
be visited: the Gothic-style hunting castle of Orlik and the
medieval Bohemian royal castle of Zvikov.

Ceske Budejovice and Hluboka Castle – A historic
town 83 miles due south of Prague, on the Vltava. Its
magnificent central square is among the largest in Europe.
Home of Budweiser beer and Koh-I-Noor pencils. Four
miles north is the romantic-type chateau of Hluboka,
rebuilt last century in the style of Windsor Castle.

In other directions, excursion possibilities include a
beer connoisseur's visit to Pilsen, to the Urquell Brewery;
to the spa town of Karlovy Vary (former Karlsbad) in the

woodlands of West Bohemia; or eastwards to the medieval silver-mining town of Kutna Hora.

The choice is rich, and there's never enough time!

5.7 Sunday in Prague

Prague has a great musical tradition which is reflected in the choral music of its many churches. Specially recommended is to attend a service at the magnificent 14th-century Tyn Church on the Old Town Square. Even more historic is the Cathedral of St Vitus, founded in 10th century. In this devout Roman Catholic country, congregations are large.

All Prague museums are open on Sunday (mostly closed Monday). Shops, banks and offices are firmly closed.

Several out-of-town excursions operate on Sundays, which can be a good day for sightseeing of castles and countryside around the capital, when the locals also are out there enjoying themselves.

5.8 Shopping in Prague

As Czechoslovakia moves towards a market economy, it's hard to predict how price levels will change. For the City Break visitor, part of the background interest comes from seeing how a country transforms from one social system to another.

The main shopping areas are in the streets radiating from the Old Town Square and around Wenceslas Square. On Celetna Street are most of the quality stores which sell gramophone records and compact discs, crystal glass, Jablonec costume jewellery and women's wear. Several beautiful shops along Na prikope and neighbouring streets sell the famous decorative coloured and cut glass, and porcelain. To see Bohemian glass of the highest quality, visit Moser at Na prikope 12.

It's fascinating to go window-shopping and pricing the goods along Wenceslas Square, which includes a number of food stores. Depending on the exchange rate when you travel, many prices may seem remarkably low. At the Supraphon music stores, for instance, reckon classical cassettes and records at £1 each. Czech wine from Southern Moravia is usually a good buy, as are the smoked meats and chocolates.

Department and clothing stores are interesting, but by West European standards the wares are utility rather than stylish. Czechoslovakia has good reputation for leather, and shoes especially are reasonably priced, though of 'sensible' style rather than high fashion. In Wenceslas Square there is enormous choice of footwear at No. 6 – the blue and white building called Dum Obuvi, which has several floors entirely devoted to shoes of every description.

In Na prikope, the department store called Detsky Dum is devoted entirely to children – clothes, toys and the like.

In many stores of the serve-yourself type, the number of customers is restrained by the number of wire baskets available. That can apply equally in a bookstore as in a shoe department. Shops are open 8-19 hrs Mon-Fri; 8-14 hrs Sat. Closed Sundays.

Tuzex shops

These stores are specifically for the purchase of goods in foreign currency or with major international credit cards. The goods are duty free, and include most Western luxury items, cigarettes and liquor. Prices are quoted in Tuzex crowns, but are readily converted into the main hard currency equivalent.

Celetna Street, leading from the Powder Tower to the Old Town Square offers the best selection of Tuzex shopping. Bohemian lead crystal shops on this street sell good quality at reasonable prices.

Other shops of interest

The USSR cultural delegation on Zelezna Street sells Soviet handicrafts, books and gramophone recordings. The Bulgarian and Hungarian shops on Na prikope likewise sell craft products, leather goods, peasant embroideries, folklore items and low-cost records and cassettes.

5.9 Eating out in Prague

There are literally hundreds of restaurants, bars and taverns in Prague. Czechs are hearty eaters. Typical meals are built around dumplings and sauerkraut, especially with pork or young goose. Fruit dumplings are popular, filled with plums or cherries. Particularly good is Prague ham, which also can appear at breakfast. For Christmas dinner – traditionally eaten on Christmas Eve – the main course is poached carp: a freshwater fish which appears year-round on lunch and dinner menus.

In the international-grade restaurants you can expect an excellent meal for £10 or less, including wine. In average restaurants £5 can easily cover a good 3-course meal. People in Prague eat early, and dining rooms close earlier than in other Continental capitals. Don't get caught out! During summer, restaurants stay open longer, but in winter they are tightly closed by 23 hrs.

All restaurants follow a 'No Smoking' policy during the busiest hours of midday till 2 p.m., and around 7 p.m. Ouside those peak hours, smoking may be permitted.

Numerous cafés are scattered all over Prague, serving a variety of cakes, rolls and drinks. Shop items like canned beer, picnic supplies or ice-cream cornets are unbelievably cheap. Stand-up self-service cafés offer very low-cost snacks, and are usually crowded.

If you prefer sitting down, the most famous cafés are clustered on Wenceslas Square (Vaclavske namesti) and other central locations. Try the cafés attached to hotels such as the Ambassador, Yalta or the Europe, and enjoy the more leisured ambiance. Look for the word *Kavarna*.

How to read the menu, if there are no clues in English? Many restaurant menus are duplicated into German. If so, you'll probably do better with the help of the German menu guide in Chapter One. Otherwise, here's a basic guide to Czech.

Soups and Starters

Bramborova	Potato soup
Gulasova	Goulash soup
Hovezi	Beef broth
Prazka sunka	Prague ham
Ruska vejce	Egg mayonnaise
Uhersky salam	Hungarian salami
Zeleninova	Vegetable soup

Main courses

Hovezi maso	Beef
Husa	Goose
Jatra	Liver
Kachna	Duck
Karbenatky	Hamburgers
Kure	Chicken
Pstruh	Trout
Rbyi filet	Fish fillet
Teleci maso	Veal
Veprove maso	Pork

Vegetarian dishes

Zelenina	Vegetables
Vejce	Eggs
Knedliky s vejci	Dumplings with scrambled eggs
Smazeny syr	Fried cheese

Vegetables and Salads

Brambory	Potatoes
Bramborovy salat	Potato salad
Hlavkovy salat	Lettuce
Hrasek	Green peas
Knedliky	Dumplings
Mrkev	Carrots
Okurkovy salat	Cucumber
Rajcatovy salat	Tomato
Ryze	Rice
Spenat	Spinach

Fruit and Desserts

Broskev	Peach
Dort	Cake, gateau
Hrusky	Pears
Jablka	Apple
Svestky	Plums
Tresne	Cherries
Ovocne knedliky	Fruit dumplings
Merunkovy	Apricot
Slehacka	Whipped cream

Drinks

Caj	Tea
Kava	Coffee
Mineralka	Mineral water
Mleko	Milk
Ovocna stava	Fruit juice
Pivo	Beer
Vino	Wine
Vinni strik	Wine with soda water
Slivovitz	Plum brandy, burns with a blue flame

Restaurant guide

All the leading hotels feature excellent international cuisine. For a high-grade meal in luxury surroundings, try the first-floor restaurant at the Palace Hotel. The price will not shatter you.

On Celetna Street in the Old Town are some very pleasing restaurants, cafés and wine-bars, several in delightful courtyards. There is a vegetarian restaurant on the first floor of No. 3 Celetna. Opposite, at No. 2, is the vinarna u Sixtu, with an attractive modern-style café on the ground floor, and a wine-cellar below which stays open till 1 a.m. Here are some more suggestions:

Pelikan Restaurant, Na prikope 7, Stare Mesto
A well-known elegant restaurant, on the first floor.
U cerveneho kone, Vodickova 36, Nove Mesto
Good food, popular restaurant.
Moskva, Na prikope 29, Stare Mesto
Russian and Georgian cuisine at reasonable prices.
Sofia, Vaclavske namesti 33, Nove Mesto
Bulgarian restaurant, very interesting.
Beograd, Vodickova 5, Nove Mesto
Yugoslavian specialities.
Rybarna, Vaclavske namesti 43, Nove Mesto
Fish specialities, particularly carp.

Beer Taverns

Czechoslovakia is understandably famed for its beer, rated as the world's best. Here are some recommended ale-houses in central Prague. Mostly they also serve meals or very substantial snacks at modest prices.

U Fleku, Kremencova 11, Nove Mesto
(At the Fleks.) Sells bitter-brewed only, Flek dark 13° beer. Excellent atmosphere. Dating from 1459, it's the oldest beer house in Prague.

U Kalicha, Na bojisti 12, Nove Mesto
(The Chalice.) Excellent food, good bar. Former haunt of the author of *Good Soldier Schweik* – a satire on war and bureaucracy. This was Schweik's favourite bar.

U supa, Celetna 22, Stare Mesto
One of the best-known Prague taverns. The speciality is Branik beer.

Hospoda U dvou kocek, Uhelny trida, Stare Mesto
(The Two Cats.) Lovely little tavern with real Prague atmosphere, and selling Pilsner Urquell 12° beer. Friendly staff with excellent service and food.

U Pinkasu, Jungmannova 15, Nove Mesto
Very popular ale-house selling Pilsner Urquell 12° beer.

U Schnellu, Tomasska 2, Mala Strana
Serves excellent food, reasonably priced.

U sv. Tomase, Letenska 12, Mala Strana
(At St Thomas's.) One of the oldest brewers, founded in 1352. Sells very good Branik dark 12° beer.

Wine bars and restaurants. Most of their wines come from Bulgaria, Yugoslavia or Hungary.

Beograd, Vodickova 5, Nove Mesto
Lobkovicka vinarna, Vlasska 17, Mala Strana
U Faustar, Karlova namesti 4, Nove Mesto
U labuti (The Swan), Hradcanske nam. 11, Hradcany
U Maliru (The Artists'), Maltezke nam. 11, Mala Strana
U patrona (The Patron), Drazickeho nam. 4, Mala Strana
Parnas-Slavia, Narodni 1, Stare Mesto
U zlate hrusky (The Golden Pear), Novy svet 3, Hradcany

5.10 Nightlife

Something for your first evening, to give a dazzling first impression of the Czech capital: find your way to the Old Town Hall Square. After-dark illuminations highlight the pastel colours with gorgeous clarity. Then stroll to Charles Bridge, which offers a superb view across the River Vltava to the brilliantly lit Jesuit church of St Nicholas Church and thence to the skyline towers of Prague Castle. The bridge itself is thronged with sightseers and entertainers.

Otherwise, much of Prague's nightlife focuses around a leisured dinner in a traditional restaurant, or among the beer-halls and wine taverns.

On the cultural circuit, Prague has an excellent ballet

company at the National Theatre and has three opera houses and five symphony orchestras. Evening programmes at theatres and concerts usually begin at 19.30 hrs. Dress is formal. If you like music, try to schedule your trip to include the Prague Spring Festival in May.

The **Laterna Magika** offers a unique theatrical experience – a remarkable mixture of dance, film, theatre and dramatic lighting effects. Try your utmost to get tickets!

Cabarets

There are many night clubs and cabarets with floor shows. Some are listed below.

Vinarna U Zelene zaby, U radnice 8, Stare Mesto
The green frog is the emblem of this wine-cellar established in 1403. One of the best wines of Czechoslovakia is sold here.

Vinarna U plebana, Betlemeske namesti, Stare Mesto
At the Plebeians – set in an historical building across from the Bethlehem Chapel – they serve Znojmo wine as the 'wine of the Bohemian kings'.

Vinarna U mecenase, Malostranske namesti 10, Mala Strana
A typical Prague wine cellar, 400 years old, with cabaret.

U Bindru, Stare Mesto
One of the oldest and most popular Prague café/cabarets, directly across from the Old Town Hall.

5.11 At your service

Money and Banking

There are 100 hellers in a Czech crown – abbreviated to Kcs. Coins are of 5, 10, 20 and 50 hellers; and 1, 2 and 5 crowns. Notes are of 10, 20, 50, 100, 500 and 1000 crowns.

Changing money

You can change at the airport, in your hotel, at a bank or at Cedok offices. Whenever you change money, it's advisable to retain the exchange docket. The official exchange rate has become 'realistic', so that most out-of-pocket expenses seem extremely cheap. Unofficial street deals that offer a 'better' rate are not worth the risk of light-fingered switching.

There are restrictions on changing back unused currency. So it's advisable to change only as much money as you expect to use. With your exchange dockets you can change back any surplus on departure.

As Czechoslovakia moves towards a free-market economy, these rules will proably be revised; so check the current regulations.

Post Office and Telephone

General Post Office, Jindriska 14, Nove Mesto

	Tel: 264841
Prague Central Station (open 24 hours)	Tel: 242544

Other Post Offices:

Namesti Republiky 8, Nove Mesto	Tel: 65818
Kaprova 12, Stare Mesto	Tel: 66707

Phone calls within Prague: Insert 1 Kcs coin, and dial number.

International calls: see dialling notes in chapter 1.3.

Emergency Telephone Numbers

First Aid	155
Ambulance	333
Dentist	261374
Police	158
Fire	150

Useful Addresses and Phone Numbers

If you have anything stolen, report it to Police Headquarters at Konviksta 14, Stare Mesto for insurance purposes. They will issue you with a declaration. You should see your travel-agency rep who will complete a report for you.

Lost Property

Kaprova 14, Stare Mesto	Tel: 60144
Bolzanova 5, Nove Mesto	Tel: 248430

Documents: Olsanska 2, Zizkov

Embassies

Great Britain, Thunovska 1, Mala Strana

	Tel: 533347
USA, Trziste 15, Mala Strana	Tel: 536641

Medical

If you see a doctor while in Prague and have to pay for the consultation, obtain a receipt both from the doctor and the chemist. This is required for claiming refund under the terms of any insurance you have. In general, medical attention is provided free of charge for British subjects.

Chemists: Emergency service at Na prikope 7

Tel: 220081

First Aid: Dukelskych hrdinu 21, Holesovice

Tel: 155

Tourist Information

Cedok, Na prikope 18	Tel: 224251
Cedok, Bilkova 6, Josefov	Tel: 2318253

Information Centre, Hradcanska Metro

Central Information Service, Na prikope 20

Tel: 544444

Which toilet door?
Toilets are marked WC or 00. Women's are labelled 'Damy' or 'Zeny'. Men's are 'Pani' or 'Muzi'.

Public holidays
January 1	New Year's Day
May 1	May Day
May 9	Czechoslovak National Day
December 25 & 26	Christmas

Easter Monday is also a public holiday.

Newspapers
In central Prague you can get the same day's Guardian, Financial Times, International Herald Tribune and Wall Street Journal – all printed on the Continent – costing 25 crowns each. Other Western newspapers and magazines arrive a day later.